W9-BQT-021

A Christmas Sampler

A Christmas Sampler
Sweet, Funny, and Strange Holiday Tales

Edited by
Sarah Fairall & Jessica Lin

Bethlehem Writers Group
Bethlehem, Pennsylvania

A CHRISTMAS SAMPLER

BWG

BETHLEHEM WRITERS GROUP

"The Perfect Gift," "Christmas Memories," "Off of the Wagon and Onto the Sleigh," and "Wisemen" copyright © 2009 by Emily P. W. Murphy
"Modern Single Holiday," "Pickle's Christmas Wonder," "Out of Season," and "Minerva" copyright © 2009 by Will Wright
"Those Things Remembered" copyright © 2009 by Paul Weidknecht (previously published in *The Oklahoma Review*)
"Visions of Sugarplum Grandmothers" copyright © 2009 by Carol A. Hanzl Birkas
"A Christmas for Johnny," "A Santa Story," and "Santa Claws" copyright © 2009 by Jerome W. McFadden
"Mis-conceptions" copyright © 2009 by Courtney Annicchiarico
"You Better Watch Out," "Nana's Chocolate Cake," and "A Christmas on Nantucket" copyright © 2009 by Carol L. Wright
"Christmas Folly" and "Christmas City Kitty" copyright © 2009 by Sally Wyman Paradysz
"Walter and Stella" copyright © 2009 by Ralph Hieb
"Auld Lang Syne" copyright © 2009 by Jo Ann Schaffer
"A Redheaded Holiday: Countdown to a Christmas Hug" copyright © 2009 by Jeff Baird
"Wishing Well Christmas" copyright © 2009 by Cindy Kelly
All images copyright © 2009 by the artist as listed on pp 233-5 and reprinted by permission of copyright holder

All rights reserved. No part of this book may be reproduced or transmitted in any form or by any means, electronic or mechanical, including photocopying, recording, or any information storage and retrieval system, without permission in writing from the copyright holder.

Simultaneous cloth and trade paperback first editions 2009

Cloth ISBN: 978-160844-111-2
Trade Paperback ISBN: 978-160844-110-5

Library of Congress Control Number applied for

Cover design copyright © 2009 by Emily P. W. Murphy
Printed in the United States of America

With gratitude
to our families and friends,
to our teachers, editors, and readers,
and to each other

The Bethlehem Writers Group is a community of mutually-supportive, fiction and nonfiction authors based in "Christmas City, USA," Bethlehem, Pennsylvania. The members are as different from each other as their stories, spanning a range of genres including: children's, young adult, paranormal, humor, inspirational, mystery, science fiction, fantasy, chick lit, romance, literary fiction, and memoir. They meet regularly to help each other refine their craft.

Table of Contents

The Perfect Gift

Emily P. W. Murphy

"*H*oney," my boyfriend, Ethan, says over coffee. "Have you given any thought to what you'd like for Christmas?"

I put down the newspaper. "No, not really. It's only September. Why?"

Ethan smiles. "Well, I know you like to shop early."

"Sure, I shop early if I think of something perfect for someone else, but I don't shop for myself."

Ethan shrugs. "I just figured if you were thinking Christmas thoughts, you might know what you wanted, and I could do my shopping early, too."

"Sorry, no such luck."

"Well, when you think of something you want, just let me know, and I'll get it."

I frown. "What do you mean by that?"

Ethan tilts his head to the side. "Huh?"

"You want me to tell you exactly what I want for Christmas, so you can just go buy it?"

Ethan nods. "That way you'll be sure to get what you want."

I shake my head. "But it doesn't work that way."

"I know it's not what we did last year. But this year we'll be at your parents' house, so in a way it'll be my first Christmas. I want to make sure I get it right."

He has a point. I hated the money clip he gave me last Christmas. The man does *not* know how to shop.

Still, he has to learn eventually. Right?

"That's sweet, honey, but don't worry so much. You can't really mess up Christmas."

"Really? Because you can mess up Hanukah. Maybe if you can't mess up Christmas you're just not trying hard enough."

I laugh. "I'm pretty sure the only way you could mess up Hanukah would be to bring me home for the Seder."

Ethan rolls his eyes. "Yeah, that would do it. Especially since that's Passover. But I'm serious, Jen. This isn't some seasonal gift exchange. It's Christmas with your parents, and I want to get it right."

I nod and decide to give the guy a break. "Okay, I'm not going to tell you what I want, because that would spoil the surprise, but I'll give you some advice. You have lots of time, so don't panic. Just remember, the gift should be a surprise, and keep in mind it'll be at my parents' house so they'll be there when I open it."

"So no edible underwear?"

"Definitely no edible underwear."

"This isn't over, Jen," he says getting up to put his dishes in the sink.

I pick the newspaper up from the table, but I can't focus on the words. What would I like for Christmas? Clothes? Books? I shake my head. There's only one thing I want for Christmas. It's the same thing I wanted, and didn't get, for my birthday and Valentine's Day and the third anniversary of our first date. The same thing I hoped to receive on Memorial Day, Flag Day, the Fourth of July, Martin Luther King Day, Earth Day, not April Fool's Day, but definitely on Presidents' Day and Cinco de Mayo. It's sparkly and comes with a four-word question. But—if I can't tell Ethan what I want for Christmas, I certainly can't tell him I want him to propose. Telling him would make it all wrong.

As much as I want to marry him, I want him to *want* to marry me. I want him to decide that it's time to go to the next level of our relationship. It has to be his idea.

***

Halloween comes and goes—no proposal. Christmas decorations appear in the stores.

"Have you figured out yet what you want for Christmas?" Ethan asks on November third as we walk past a plastic North Pole set up in the middle of the mall. A skinny Santa with a fake beard is already sitting in the oversized throne, and eager children are lining up to have their pictures taken.

"Yes," I say giving Ethan what I hope is a sly look. "I know what I want, but I'm not going to tell you."

Ethan frowns. "Why not?"

"Because it has to be a surprise."

Ethan stops walking and turns to me. "Wait, I have to be surprised by what you want me to give you for Christmas?"

"No." I roll my eyes. "I have to be surprised by what you're giving me. Otherwise, what's the point?"

"The point is you'll get something you like."

"We've been dating for years; I'm sure you can come up with something I'd like."

He nods and thinks for a while, then looks toward the North Pole. "Would you tell him what you want?" he asks pointing to the Santa.

I glance at the display, and then back at Ethan. "What, so you can listen in?"

Ethan winks. "Then you wouldn't be telling me . . . so it's not cheating."

I shake my head. "Surprise me."

***

13

Thanksgiving comes and goes with no proposal. I remind myself to be thankful that Ethan cares for me, but it is hard not to wonder whether he's avoiding a permanent commitment.

"Here you go," Ethan says, coming into our bedroom on the evening of December first. I put down the book I am reading and take the sheet of paper he holds out to me.

"What's this?" I ask, looking at the typed page.

"It's my Christmas list."

I frown and read the list. "What's with number seven?" I ask. "Kitchen trash can with foot pedal?"

"Yeah, one that you step on the pedal and it opens for you, you know?"

"Yeah, I know, but I'm not getting you one for Christmas."

"Why not? It's on my list."

"You're not three, and I'm not Santa Claus. I don't have to stick to some silly list. And even if I were to get something from the list, a trash can is a lousy present."

"It's a nice trash can."

"It's a trash can; it's meant to hold trash!"

"Nice trash?"

"Giving you a trash can is no way to celebrate the birth of our Lord and Savior."

"*Your* Lord and Savior."

"Whatever. If you want a trash can, go buy one. You're not getting it for Christmas."

Ethan shrugs. "There's lots of other stuff on the list."

I read the rest of his list. "Why do you need virus protection software?"

"I have some money saved up, so I'm buying a new laptop. It will need to be protected."

I frown. I thought he might use that money for a ring. "What do you need a new laptop for?"

"Mine is four years old; it's too slow."

I feel my patience evaporating. "Are you sure this is the best time to spend so much on a computer?"

Ethan shrugs. "Why not?"

I hand him back his list. "I don't need this."

***

On Pearl Harbor Day, Ethan pulls the list out of his pocket and tries to hand it back to me as we walk through the grocery store.

"I've added a few things," he says.

"I won't take it," I say, shaking my head. He shrugs and sticks it in my purse. I choose to ignore him rather than make a scene in the cereal aisle.

"I've made things easy for you now, so you have to help me out. What do you want?"

"No," I say a bit too loud. A woman with a toddler glances in our direction. I lower my voice and turn away from her. "Listen, if you're so worried, then you can always ask my mom for ideas."

"Your mom?" Ethan throws a box of Cheerios into the cart.

"Yeah, she knows me pretty well. I'm sure she'll have a good idea."

"You want me to ask your mom what I should get you for Christmas?"

"Yeah, why not?"

"I can just imagine what she'd say you need."

"What's that?"

"A nice, Catholic boyfriend."

"Don't be ridiculous—we're Episcopalian. Besides, Mom loves you."

"This would be the same mother who made me sleep in the basement when we visited for Thanksgiving?"

I shrug. "Her house, her rules. We're not married, and that's the way it has to be. What's so bad about the basement?"

"It's unfinished!"

I suppress a smile. "You had an inflatable mattress and a space heater. It could have been worse." I don't mention that the basement was my idea. Mom probably would have let him sleep in the living room.

***

Once the groceries are put away, I sneak off to take a good look at his Christmas list. It's extensive. Great, now I have to come up with something not on this list. He's asked for every book, CD, and DVD I would have thought of. He's certainly making things difficult.

***

On December fifteenth, he asks again in the car on the way to his office Christmas party. "What's a good, traditional Christmas present?"

I sigh. "Still don't know what to get me?"

He shrugs. "Maybe, maybe not. I'm just curious."

He's a bad liar. "Gold, frankincense, and myrrh," I say, looking out the passenger-side window.

We drive in silence for a moment, the windshield wipers squelching a staccato rhythm.

"What the hell is frankincense?" he asks at last.

I turn back to him and shrug. "Who knows? What the hell is myrrh?"

***

"I know what I'm getting you," he says on December twentieth.

"Good for you. Now don't tell me."

"Oh, I won't. It'll be a complete surprise. I just have to order it."

An hour later he walks into the kitchen where I am mixing up a batch of Christmas cookies. He holds up an old sneaker of mine.

"Jen, does this sneaker fit you?" he asks.

My hopes crash down around me. "Subtle," I mutter.

"Huh?"

"Nothing. Yeah, they fit fine." I pause, then decide to make him squirm. "Why?"

Ethan shuffles his feet. "I, uh, thought I'd clean out the closet, and if these didn't fit, I figured I'd donate them to Goodwill or something."

"Ah, of course."

***

I decide to get him a laptop case for his new computer. I hate that computer, but I love Ethan. Besides, it's the only thing that isn't on that stupid list. On December twenty-second, I find the perfect case online. So much for shopping early. I order it and pay extra for the overnight shipping.

The next day, I hurry home early from work to pick up the mail. I don't want Ethan to see his gift before Christmas. There is a package waiting on the front porch, but it looks too small for a laptop case. I check the return address. DiscountEShoes.com. I sigh, leave the box on the stoop, and go into the house. I try to ignore the shoebox when Ethan brings it into the house, but it's hard since he "hides" it on our closet shelf.

His laptop case arrives later that night, just in time for me to wrap it and add it to our pile of luggage for the trip. Ethan is in the shower when it arrives, so I work quickly.

***

The next morning, Christmas Eve, we pack the car together. Ethan raises an eyebrow when he sees my gift for him, wrapped in bright Christmas paper. "That's not a trash can," he says.

"No," I say. "It's not."

He shrugs and puts the shoebox, unwrapped, into the trunk. I pretend not to notice.

Holiday traffic makes the drive to my parents' house longer than usual. We spend most of the time in silence. I am too annoyed to make small talk, so I pump up the Christmas carols on the radio. "You better not pout," Bing Crosby reminds me. I sigh and turn the radio down.

When we arrive at my parents' house, we change and go with them to church. I look at Ethan, all dressed up for the occasion. He looks dashing.

He gives me a lopsided grin. "You think God will mind I'm Jewish?"

I laugh, remembering why I love him. "I'm pretty sure he's okay with the Chosen People. Jesus was Jewish, too, you know."

"That's a terrible thing to say," he says winking.

The Christmas Eve service opens with my favorite hymns. We sing together with the congregation, our voices filling the nave. Ethan hums the parts he doesn't know, but, for a guy who has never been to church, he does great. We sit holding hands through the scripture reading, and I remember how thankful I am that he's supportive of my faith.

The priest takes the pulpit and delivers the Christmas Eve homily. "Christmas is a time when we show our appreciation of others," he says. "It is a time when we give gifts, just as Christ gave us the ultimate gift of eternal life. It can be easy to get caught up in the shopping and gifting, but we must not forget Our Father and all of His gifts. He says 'ask and ye shall be given' . . ."

Ethan nudges my ribs with his elbow, and I stifle a laugh. I was definitely too hard on him. I resolve to love the sneakers when I open them in the morning. He tried hard, and deserves my appreciation. I bite my lip, hoping he'll like his gift, too.

The service closes with "Silent Night." The lights go down, and we all sing in candlelight.

"Go in peace to love and serve the Lord," the priest says when the last notes die away. "And Merry Christmas."

"Thanks be to God," we all respond.

***

The next morning we gather around the Christmas tree. I look at my family. My parents, married for thirty-five years, my brother and his wife and their two children, and Ethan—all together this Christmas morning. I smile. No Christmas could be more perfect.

When it is my turn to open my first gift, I pick up the shoebox, now wrapped in tacky birthday paper. "Can I open this now?" I ask.

Ethan shakes his head. "No, it's too good; you should wait."

I laugh, and open a gift from my dad.

Ethan picks up my gift to him. "This one?" he asks, looking at me. I nod.

"Yeah, open it now. I hope you like it."

It's a nice laptop case, but it's not something he asked for. He'll probably like the gifts from my family better since I gave them the list.

He picks at the tape.

"Rip it!" my brother yells, just like he did when we were kids.

"But it's so nicely wrapped," Ethan protests.

"Rip it, rip it," the kids chant.

"Rip it, rip it," I join in.

"Rip it, rip it, rip it," my parents cheer.

Ethan laughs and, taking one corner of the paper, rips it lengthwise along the box. He tosses the paper aside and flips the box over to inspect the picture.

"This wasn't on the list," he says.

I swallow. "No, sorry. I hope that's okay."

He looks up at me and his expression is one of awe.

"It's perfect," he breathes. "I love it. How did you know?"

I smile. "I have a lot of experience Christmas shopping," I say, relieved.

"I guess I have a lot to learn," he says, flashing me that lopsided grin. "Teach me, sensei."

**

Several more rounds of gift giving pass, and still Ethan insists that I wait to open his gift. I love how much he's getting into the celebration, even chanting "rip it, rip it," when my mom starts picking at a piece of tape.

Finally, the shoebox is the only gift I have left. I pick it up and shake it, hearing the shoes clunk inside. "Now can I open it?"

Ethan makes a show of considering my question, then nods. "Yeah, I think you've waited long enough. I tear the paper open to reveal the Nike box.

"Sneakers!" I cry. "How did you know?"

Ethan grins. "Remember when I asked you whether those ratty sneakers in the closet still fit?"

I pretend to think back. "Ye-eah," I say nodding as

though it is a vague memory but I do remember it, now that he mentions it.

"Well, I saw how old those were and knew you'd need a new pair." He grins, clearly proud of his deductive skills. "And," he says with a flourish, "I got them for a really good price."

I laugh and pull the lid off the shoebox. The sneakers are grey and yellow, and at least two sizes too big. God, they're ugly.

"I love them," I say, resolving to exchange them for an identical pair in the correct size.

"Try them on," Ethan says.

"Right now?"

"Yeah, I can't wait to see how they look."

I bite my lip. I bet, if I tie the laces really tight, he won't even notice they're too big.

I shrug. "Okay, why not?"

I pull out the first shoe. With everyone watching, I struggle to loosen the laces. *What was he thinking when he bought these?* I reach in and pull out the paper stuffing in the toe. It wasn't as much as I had expected to find in such an enormous sneaker. I start to put the shoe on, but my toe hits more wadding.

"Sorry," I say, looking at Ethan whose grin now seems mixed with a level of anticipation far beyond anything these shoes deserve. I pick up the sneaker, and reach in again. A tear forms in my eye as I look at Ethan and realize that my fingers are touching a tiny velvet box.

Modern Single Holiday

Headley Hauser

We wish you a merry humbug. We wish you a merry humbug—maybe I covered that in the first sentence.

Single men get labeled (unfairly) as Scrooge-like when it comes to the holidays. While it's true that Ebenezer was a bachelor, it would be unreasonable to say that he was typical of our type.

First of all, Ebenezer hardly lived alone. He had four ghosts in residence, including his Rasta ex-business partner, Jacob Bob Marley. Secondly, the man had servants and never once slept in an unmade bed or ate a bag of microwave popcorn for dinner. Finally, I can't think of a third reason, but who ever heard of a position without three points?

You might think that just because single men throw Christmas cards away unopened and snarl at shopping mall Santas, that we lack an appreciation for holiday spirit. What you fail to take into account is that we, the unwashed denizens of studio apartments, have legitimate holiday traditions of our own.

Now, please remember that tolerance begins with appreciating the differences of others. Single men are rarely PC (at heart), but we have no qualms about invoking such tripe on others. So, stuff that judgmental attitude where the sun don't shine and enter the world of the Bachelor Winter Wonderland.

Deck the halls with dirty laundry. What? Surely, you're not so close-minded as to insist on pretty lights, peppermint sticks, and frosted Dollar Store figurines to make a home festive? A chair is just a chair, but a chair with blue jeans, jockey shorts, and one odd sock is a festooned celebration of peace on Earth and good will 'til laundry day.

I've always taken great comfort in that old favorite: *God rest ye single gentlemen, and sleep through church this day. At night they light the candles, so wait for the display. To save us in that darkened hour so we can slip away, without bindings or promises of toil: promise of toil. Such as deacon work, our holiday to spoil.*

Of course there's the twelve days of Christmas (in the sink). *On the twelfth day of Christmas my scrub sink held for me: twelve spoons from coffee, eleven knives from toffee, ten forks spaghetti, nine pans Crocker Betty, eight cups a-soakin', seven dishes broken, six things best-not-spoken, five drops of Joy (la–la–la), four Tupperware, three sauce pans, two really grungy pads, and a crock pot I got from Aunt Marge.*

Let's pause a minute in the midst of our euphoric gaiety and salute the very reason our kind survives, sometimes for decades, past college graduation: the female relative. If it weren't for Aunt Marge, Mom, Sis, Grandma, Niece and Soft-hearted-neighbor-lady-who-adopts-strays, your average bachelor would be eating wet sawdust on the floor before his twenty-eighth birthday. (I mention twenty-eight because that's the year most women, quite correctly, recognize that the bachelor, so appealing in years past, has now spoiled liked a soft cantaloupe and will never be trainable as a proper husband.) These noble women (if you're having trouble following this paragraph, just ignore all parenthetical asides) provide edible food and helpful laundry tips in sufficiently frequent intervals to keep bachelors from such feral acts as eating raw tuna-helper while peeing in the shower. (Only the ignored single man does both at the same time.) Their visits to the bachelor's home ensure that he will wash (or throw out) the dishes, do his laundry, and hide debris regularly.

Back to traditions.

Oh little mound of Doritos bags, how still I see thee lie. On my trash heap and way down deep in my laundry not yet dry. Yet with your sparkling presence, your green and red doth glow. When from my seat, I see none to eat; to the convenience store, I go. For Christmas, many single men turn to the hot Doritos. If the trashcan, like a merry heart, is overflowing, it just makes sense that bags should be green as well as red. It's not that we want to eat Doritos actually; it's that we know they are so nutritionally balanced. There's nacho cheese (dairy), corn (grain) hot peppers (fruits and veggies) and the hydrogenated animal fat (distant cousin to protein).

Away in a futon, no room on his bed. The cherubic bachelor with dreams in his head. That Jesus and Santa will work side by side. And bring him an X-box and a Porsche-a to ride.

Of course, we know that Jesus was born a baby, ignorant of social customs and incapable of caring for his own needs. Sound like someone you know? Perhaps we, the full-sized infants known as single men, expose our pathetic ineptitude during the holiday season as a public service.

Or maybe we're just hoping that Scrooge's ghosts will stop by and tidy up a bit.

Those Things Remembered

Paul Weidknecht

The beard was key. Of this, Ralph was certain. Anyone could put on the suit and cap, but the beard was the trademark, the thing that pulled the whole look together. A natural brilliant white, it had been that way before his retirement from the plant seven years ago, where even the guys on the job called him Santa. He was convinced this was the reason for that wonder in children's eyes when they sat on Santa's lap. Even shy kids who had to be coaxed up to the throne, who'd bury their chins in their chests as if they'd forgotten their lines for the school play, nearly always managed a sideways peek at the beard, amazed at its ethereal look. And the ones who didn't need coaxing, the bold ones, they'd sometimes give it a tug for proof. Except for babies, every kid could discern a real one from a fake. This hair was also why the Fairbridge Mall had hired him for the last seven seasons to be their guy in red.

Black Friday, the day after Thanksgiving, and the indoor city of Fairbridge Mall bustled. Sounds of clicking shoes, rustling bags, and shouting children bounced off the hard floor, mixed and overlapped, filling the mall. This may have been noise to others, but Ralph never heard it that way: it was the sound of an orchestra warming up before the curtain rises. As Ralph settled deeply into his leather chair at the center of the atrium, watching the children and parents queue around the base of his kingdom, he had to admit the mall really went all out this year. The set-up *was* impressive. Frosted in plastic snow, the new castle stood over an expanse of white felt speckled with glittering sequins. Nearby sat a full-sized antique sleigh piled high with a mound of prop gifts, empty boxes wrapped in metallic red, green and silver paper. The canted heads of robotic reindeer scanned dumbly back and forth, as mechanical elves waved, the entire scene illuminated with blue and pink lights for that North Pole look. No red bow stapled to a plywood riser for Fairbridge.

Despite the fine work of the mall carpenters, Ralph was never fully persuaded that the Christmas season started the day after Thanksgiving. With yesterday's turkey still not fully digested, it seemed rushed to start in on another holiday. The weather didn't seem right either; it needed to be colder. He recalled his youth in the north woods of Maine, where it seemed everyone had half a backyard dedicated to a winter's supply of firewood, where every single day in December saw the ground covered in snow, and there was always a chance of snow falling on December twenty-fifth. Here, snow didn't exist in November, was rare in December, and a Christmas Eve snowfall was like hitting a meteorological lottery.

But he was an actor who disappeared into the role. People new to the business always forgot things, and professionals always carried extras. White gloves. Santa had to have them when holding the reins. Reading spectacles, the wire-rimmed, rectangular ones. Santa had to read the list. Even breath mints. Kids had no problem asking Santa for a radio-controlled car and telling him he had bad breath in the same sitting.

But he wasn't sure why he'd been distracted by the thought of his beard, or about Maine. It wasn't like him to have his mind filled up with other things while working.

He had another problem. And it had absolutely nothing to do with the fact he had not been relieved for his lunch break, or that he was burning up inside the heavy suit because the mall had forgotten to provide a fan. Even the fact that his left pant leg had been dampened by not one, but two children in the past forty-five minutes wasn't something he couldn't handle.

The real problem concerned this last little girl, the one who'd just had the accident. The accident was no big deal, a hazard of the job, but he had forgotten her name. *Forgotten* it. That hadn't happened before. Ever. Parents, even mall managers, were quick to detect an impersonal Santa Claus, and the ones who couldn't connect with kids by remembering names and gift requests soon found themselves not being Saint Nick anymore.

She had told him her name, and suddenly the name was gone, lost in a thousand other possibilities. Whenever a child would tell him a name, he would repeat it and imagine the first letter stamped onto the center of the kid's forehead. What it lacked in warmth, it made up for in function, and, until now, the trick had never failed him.

Time passed and Ralph got his lunch break, changing into a dry pair of pants between bites. Although the manager rolled his eyes at the request, eventually he ended up with a box fan someone found buried in a storeroom, making the last hour of the shift tolerable.

***

Rain slanted across Ralph's headlights as he drove slowly past the rows of cars, picking his way through the mall lot. He tapped the brakes, allowing a pair of teenagers to sprint in front of him. Someone behind him blasted a horn, shouting something through a half-opened window as Ralph moved on toward the exit, to the boulevard and the interstate. Fifteen minutes later, suburban streets, already glittering with decorations, gave way to black rural roads, where lack of the same made it seem as if the season were still six months away. The dotted centerline reflected brilliant yellow against the night, as the car rushed through the closing fog, pushing it to both sides. Glancing up into the rearview mirror, Ralph saw a white glow hanging over the mall miles behind.

He wasn't sick, but he didn't feel like he normally would after work. This season seemed hurried, impersonal, not at all like the others. The manager was new, a young guy, not the person who had been there previous seasons. Whenever he and Ralph spoke, the man appeared distracted, his gaze constantly drifting behind Ralph, the kind of person who nods a lot and hears only half of anything that bores him. Ralph was suspicious of these young, middle-management types. They were the kind who stepped into a situation, making changes for the sake of creating something new. To these folks, changes could only be improvements.

Taking this job had been a compromise between Eleanor and Ralph, a halfway point, with neither getting everything, but both getting something. Ralph wanted to stay on at the plant; Eleanor wouldn't hear of it. To her thinking, Ralph had done his time and was deserving of his pension the very moment he qualified for it. Sixty-five was the end of the race, the finish line, not an opportunity to lose it all by running another stretch. She'd heard too many stories of men overstaying their welcome, union paychecks too fat to leave for the next person in line, dying at their machines, each becoming a cautionary tale for those who would consider suckling the company past their weaning.

Had Eleanor forgiven him? After these years he was still unsure. Their savings—the money that was supposed to buy Eleanor's dream house in Florida— had evaporated, slowly disappearing as he insisted on playing financial planner. When it was finally gone, with no chance of a market turn-around or recovery, he realized his stubbornness had also ensured him a lifetime of labor. Whether as a plant foreman or mall Santa, Ralph knew he would need to work until the dirt hit the casket. The pension and Social Security would pay the bills, keep the grandchildren in gifts, but the dream house in Florida would remain just that, a dream.

He looked to the side of the road; a speed limit sign whipped past. Something about it wasn't right; the sign was too tilted, the numbers and letters not as black and sharp as they should've been, the white background too ashy. This road was suddenly unfamiliar to him, and it was only when he'd reached the ancient gas station at the crossroads eight miles later that he realized he'd taken a wrong turn, something he couldn't remember ever doing in the last thirty-two years. He turned into the gas station, swung through the lot, and drove home.

***

Time had moved faster than Ralph had expected, and he found it hard to believe it was already December seventeenth. As he changed into his costume in the employee locker room, Ralph reached into his gym bag and grabbed a bottle of Vitamin C. He popped two tablets, then thought better and popped another two. If tonight was going to be like any other night, he'd be coughed at and sneezed on at least two dozen times before the shift ended. Just a shade over a week and that would be it for another year. Soon Eleanor would begin packing for their trip.

By now the trip was ritual. For the past seven years they had gone to Florida to visit Eleanor's sister. They'd leave by noon on Christmas Day and arrive in south Florida three days later, staying for a month. Kaye and Tom would try to talk them into staying at their home, but they always declined, choosing instead a nearby rental. The two couples would spend the day together and go out for dinner in the evening. Afterwards, they'd part ways, two returning to a home with no mortgage, two withdrawing to something else. Ralph's Santa money covered the rental, but whenever they'd wave goodbye until the next morning, he never forgot that a month in a Florida rental was not a home in Florida.

So many times during their drive back north, he would turn toward Eleanor and try to guess what she was thinking. Much of the time she stared dully out at the interstate, expressionless. Every so often a billboard advertising senior living would pass, showing happy, fit, silver-haired couples in pastel colors, with impossibly white dentures, their arms around each other, strolling contentedly, maybe with a golf course in the background. Golden years under golden sunshine. Ralph never had the heart to examine her face, to study it for a meaning. Was she tired? Was she sad that the vacation was ending? Or was she regretful of a life that hadn't matched her expectations?

Ralph remembered his courting days, of standing in the foyer of Eleanor's huge house under a chandelier that cost more than his father made in a year. While her mother went to find Eleanor, her father sat in the living room staring at him, saying nothing, rolling a cigar between his lips with his thumb and forefinger. Smoke curled above his head, and every so often he would exhale with his mouth wide, blowing out a cloud that obscured his entire face. The act was vulgar, and every time it happened, Ralph reasoned the old man did it to shield himself from the young man who was sure to drag his daughter into poverty with the ridiculous notion that love was more important than money.

It took several decades, but it seemed the old man had been right.

***

His Santa show started the moment he emerged from the employee area. He walked to the castle waving and laughing. A string of children who'd managed to twist free from their parent's grips followed, some skipping, others pointing out their discovery to anyone willing to look.

Within an hour he had forgotten three names. The fan had disappeared and he pulled a handkerchief from a side pocket to wipe his brow. An actor has to stay in character regardless of the variables, he thought. Always take a good picture. Smile. Keep the twinkle in the eye. Try to remember the names, if not, then get the gift request right.

The manager showed up several hours later while Ralph took his second break. The kid handed Ralph his timecard and he suddenly remembered that morning; he'd been late. He had accidentally entered Fairbridge through the far entrance. The mistake cost him a long walk and six extra minutes.

The kid stood before him in an inexpensive, white, single-ply shirt and blue tie. Any business look he may have been trying to effect was lost by the fact he wasn't wearing a T-shirt and that his chest and stomach were visible under the thin cloth.

"You've been with us for a while, Ralph, so—"

"I've been here for seven years. This is my eighth."

The kid nodded slowly and frowned. "Right. Well, we've had some problems with lateness and I have to address it. Everyone, whether they've been here eight years or eight days needs to show up on time." The kid produced a folder and opening it, withdrew a sheet of paper. "This is an oral warning."

"It doesn't look like an oral warning," Ralph said. "It looks like a written warning."

"No, it's an oral warning. Oral warnings have to be documented. A written warning would come next."

"Doesn't *oral* imply something being done by verbal instruction, hence the name—oral?"

"Like I said, an oral warning has to be documented."

"So a written warning should really be a written-written warning. Or maybe a double-written warning. You know, they really should change the terminology on these things. It could get confusing for someone who's not as informed as yourself," Ralph said, smiling.

The kid swallowed and his eyes narrowed. "I hope you're not confused anymore, Ralph."

"I am, actually. I'm confused as to why an employee—a senior—doesn't have the fan he requested. I'm confused as to why I don't always get my break as required by law. OSHA doesn't like people getting picked on, especially us old ones."

The kid rolled his eyes. "Ralph, no one is picking on you. And regarding the warning, you have the choice of signing this or not. By signing it, you are not agreeing with it, only acknowledging that we have discussed it."

"You can keep it. My gift," Ralph said, grinning. "Merry Christmas."

***

Driving to the mall, Ralph was grateful the twenty-fourth had arrived. The month had been long.

The interstate curved and rose, giving Ralph a view of the passing town as if looking down on a miniaturized scene, the scale somewhere between that of a model train platform and real life, making it seem more manageable. Still, he shook his head. It was far from manageable. Everything had exploded over the past seven years. Even before that. What had been stretches of unbroken woods was now a jumble of box stores, hotels, electronics outlets, hardware megastores, and gourmet burger chains. Parcels of land yet unoccupied sat as dirt, marked by bulldozers and dump trucks and piles of uprooted trees, a developer's placard with name and number facing out from the scalped lot. Roads and ramps, underpasses and overpasses, business routes and service roads. Ralph wondered if there was a saturation point. How many different toppings for burgers could there possibly be? And how many people *needed* new toppings for burgers? Yet Ralph still knew that without this development, Fairbridge wouldn't exist, and if Fairbridge didn't exist, neither would his job.

Traffic was heavy and he found himself pinned in the fast lane. He flicked on his turn signal and worked his way over, lane by lane, finally veering from the roadway with one quick turn onto the exit just in front of a tractor trailer, the bark of its air horn startling Ralph as he curved slowly around the ramp. He saw the mall in the distance.

He parked and grabbed his gym bag from the seat beside him. As he approached the entrance, he could see garland, lights, shoppers. He stepped inside the door and stopped short.

Nothing was the same. Nothing. The castle was gone. No sparkling white felt. There were no robotic reindeer, no elves, no gifts in a sleigh. A skinny teenager wearing a fake beard, and a pillow under his coat, sat in a vinyl easy chair. Cottony stuffing sprouted from tears in both arms and the headrest. Twin infants sat teetering on each knee, crying as their mother tried to take a picture between sobs. Three mothers stood waiting in line with four kids.

Ralph turned to the left. No gourmet pretzel shop. And down from it, no record store. Instead he saw a sports shop and a clothing store for teen girls. He looked to the right. No puppies in shredded newspaper jumping from behind a glass partition, just a place selling fruit drinks, things he thought they called smoothies. Down from it was another girls' clothing boutique, but no jewelry store. Everything was wrong.

He felt himself walk back to the car, each step wavering and uncertain. He was dizzy and could feel sweat warm on the back of his neck. His bag now felt heavy and he wanted to drop it in the middle of the parking lot and keep going, unburdened by anything extra.

Then he remembered, not what he wanted to remember, but something that had just worked itself to the surface. The memory was good, and he found comfort in its suddenness, that some part of his mind was functioning, and that it could call up something so vivid.

One particular Christmas Eve in Maine, as a boy, he'd walked out onto the back porch after dusk, the rush of air sudden and cold on his face and hands. With the snow past his knees, he punched step after step through the hard crust, trudging to the center of the yard and turning. Over the entrance to his father's workshop, the silhouette of antlers from a moose taken years before rose dark and bony against the blue twilight. Then the door creaked, the wind moving it in and out against latch and lock. He looked back at the house. The dining room light shone over the snow's glazed surface, and occasionally he'd see his mother or father pass by the window making preparations for

the evening. Inside, their tree stood trimmed and sparkling, all of it as inviting and warm and real as anything he had ever experienced in his short life. They would go to church later that night, come home to sleep, and wake to Christmas.

He recalled knowing he would remember this moment. He'd take a snapshot of it in his mind, more real than anything on film, remembering it as long as he lived. He couldn't think of a better Christmas Eve.

And now he couldn't think of one worse. He was suddenly bitter, and he smiled at the irony: Santa Claus lost on Christmas Eve. What was more useless than a Santa Claus who couldn't remember kid's names or what they wanted? One who couldn't find the chimney.

***

As Eleanor lighted a scented candle in the front window, a police car pulled up out front. A moment passed before she realized it was a state trooper and not the local police. A jolt went through her stomach. Behind the driver's side window, the police officer's head tilted downward as if writing something on the steering wheel. He turned toward the house, looking at it from behind black oval sunglasses. Eleanor felt her legs go weak. She reached out and placed her palms on the table that held the candle.

The trooper stepped from the cruiser and opened the rear door. Ralph emerged from the back seat with his head down and offered his hand still looking at the ground. The officer shook it and handed him something. Ralph watched the car pull away, as he slowly made his way up the front walk carrying his gym bag.

Eleanor held the door open, but as he squeezed past her, he didn't look up. Relief and fear and questions swirled through her mind, but she couldn't seem to speak. His face showed things, said things, that went beyond words or comfort or simple explanations. She followed him into the dining room, and they sat at the table. He handed her a business card.

"That's the trooper's card," he said, motioning toward it. "On the back. He wrote it all down."

She flipped it over, shaking her head. "What's this?"

"That's where our car is now."

"Orchard Mills Mall. JC Penney. Lot B." Eleanor muttered the words. "I don't understand."

Ralph let out a breath, looking up at the ceiling, then closed his eyes. "I got lost on the way to the mall. I was going to work and got off at the wrong exit. Pretty soon, I was at Orchard Mills, lost. More than lost."

She wanted to ask him the obvious, why he hadn't just gotten back on the interstate, taken the correct exit, and gone to work; but she wasn't sure she wanted to hear the answer.

"Eleanor, I took the wrong exit thinking it was the right one. I pulled up to Orchard Mills thinking it was Fairbridge. I even walked inside. Got more confused than ever. I came back out to the car and sat for an hour not knowing what to do. The trooper drove by and I flagged him down." Ralph threw his hands up. "I'm just sorry."

"For what?"

"Sorry for all of it. The bad decisions. The things I wasn't able to give you. The Florida house."

She leaned forward, taking his hand. His face was flushed, red. He looked away. She let his hand go and pulled him into her with both arms around his shoulders.

"Oh, Ralph, it was never about things. You should know that. It was always about us. I don't care about houses in Florida or anywhere else. I'm happy now, the way things are. Do you think I'd ever want a place anywhere without you?"

"No," he said with his head down.

"You're the most important person in my life. It's always been that way, and always will be. We're in this together, no matter what happens," she said.

"I have an idea," Eleanor continued. "Let's go to church tonight. Let's spend Christmas Eve together like we used to."

They hadn't been to church on Christmas Eve for seven years, with Ralph hopelessly wrung-out, his energy always spent as the job came to an end for another year. The candlelight part of the service, when a single flame was taken from the altar and passed along to every person in the church, each holding a small white candle, was their favorite. The lights would dim, the sanctuary illuminated in amber, each person's face aglow, everyone singing "Silent Night." They'd file from the church, shake hands with the pastor, renewed and reminded that no matter what gifts were given the next morning or what wishes realized, their gift of Christ had already been given a long time ago.

"I'd like that," he said.

The phone rang and neither of them moved. On the fifth ring the answering machine kicked on. It was the Fairbridge kid. His voice was measured and tense, his annoyance clear with each breath he drew through his nose. They listened as he instructed Ralph to see him in his office first thing tomorrow morning, then to his stammering as he remembered it would be Christmas morning, and rescheduling the meeting for the twenty-sixth.

Eleanor smiled and leaned into her husband, her forehead pressed to his. "Ralph, I think you just got fired."

"Isn't that terrible," Ralph said, smiling back.

An hour went by before Ralph walked into the bathroom and climbed out of his coat, letting it drop from his shoulders like a backpack shed by a trail-worn hiker. Lowering the lid onto the toilet seat, he sat down and pulled off his boots. He stayed there, slumped for a moment, his belly filling the space between his chest and thighs, then gave the boots a lazy kick to the side and looked out the window. Snow was beginning to fall in large goose-down flakes, and he could see them melt slowly on the birdfeeder's tiny black roof. He stood up and stared into the medicine cabinet mirror.

He'd never given much credence to the idea of the mirror revealing something about him he didn't already know. That sort of thing was for people with too little insight and too much imagination. But now he had to admit that he did look different, or maybe he just felt different.

Opening the medicine cabinet, he looked from shelf to shelf, and after scrounging around for a moment, getting what he wanted, he pushed the door closed. He threw the tiny lever under the sink faucet, closing the stopper. *How much time do any of us have left,* he thought. *Ten years? A year? The next half-hour?* Love over things. It seemed so obvious now. He remembered taking the job because of compromise, and now it seemed that leaving because of love was just a normal course of what was inevitable, maybe fateful. Because of this, it didn't feel sentimental or strange or frightening when the quiet snip came, followed by a tuft of white hair—not that ethereal after all—falling silently into the sink.

Visions of Sugarplum Grandmothers

Carol A. Hanzl Birkas

"Tiny little Baby, tiny little Baby, tiny little Baby born in Beth-le-hem."

My thirteen-year-old granddaughter was practicing for an upcoming Christmas pageant. She was performing her own concert, reggae style, for me over the telephone. Performing for Gramma has always been one of her favorite things to do, and her "shows" have been the highlight of many a day for me. We have a special bond, my Jessi and I.

Christmas season, 2008, was upon us, and she was quite caught up in it. Christmas in our family is a magical time. Our tree goes up the day after Thanksgiving, and we don't take it down until well into January. During that glorious interlude, Christmas lives in our hearts and in our homes.

The "Tiny Little Baby" song took me back in time to another Christmas and a different tiny little baby. It was Jessi's first Christmas, and it was the first Christmas that I celebrated as a grandmother. I remember it well. . . .

***

I was sitting in my rocking chair with my precious three-month-old granddaughter in my arms. She was spending the night at Gramma's, and I was in my

43

glory. The setting was perfect. The spice-scented candles burning on the mantle and the warm glow of the Christmas tree lights lent the only illumination to the room. Christmas music was turned down low, and I softly sang along as I rocked my baby. Her big, brown eyes were wide open, and as I gazed into them in wonder, they stared intently right back at me. A feeling of pure contentment came over me. My heart was filled to overflowing with love for this child, and, as I studied her little face, I was positive that she was getting as much out of this as I was.

We sat there for a long time that way. As I rocked her, I started to think about my own grandmothers. Were they anywhere near as enchanted with me as I was with this tiny being? Did they ever hold me like this? I was sure they must have. I know they loved me, and I loved them dearly, but I could not remember ever having this kind of connection with either of them. I had childhood friends who were extremely close to their grandmothers. I envied them in secret for having that special relationship. My own children were very fortunate. They were blessed with grandmothers on both sides who were absolutely perfect.

Reflecting on this, I began feeling sorry for the little girl that I was. *I really missed out on a lot*, I thought, and, as I lowered my eyes to my now sleeping bundle, I remember thinking quite smugly, *Oh, but so did they!*

As I sat there, rocking and licking my wounds while staring absently into the lights on the tree, one of the lights seemed to flicker a little more brightly than the rest. Startled, I watched as it glowed even brighter, and then took on a life of its own as it detached itself from the tree. I stared in amazement as a Sugarplum Fairy ornament floated across the room and perched herself delicately upon my knee, right above Jessi's head.

"I am the spirit of your Mom-mom." She spoke gently in my Mom-mom's voice. "I hear what you are thinking, and I came to tell you that I did love you very much. And yes, I did sit with you, many times, that exact same way. You cannot possibly remember; you were much too young. I want you to know that when we were together, every moment was special to me, and when you were not with me physically, you were always in my heart. I wish so much that I could have conveyed this to you back then. My life was so different from yours; it was a lot more complex.

"You see dear, you were my fourth grandchild—not my first. Now that does not mean that I loved you any less. It simply means that I was spread a lot more thin. I did not have the luxury at that time of being able to cultivate a single flower, so to speak. You are fortunate to be in a position that enables you to do just that. I had a garden of little flowers by the time you came along, and I loved them all. I nurtured them in the best way I knew how. Unfortunately, dear, in my beautiful garden, there were some ugly, overpowering weeds. There was one in particular that, no matter how I tried, I could not eradicate. These weeds grew so tall and so thick that, eventually, I was not able to enjoy my flowers because the weeds kept getting in the way."

It was at that moment that a second fairy chose to make her entrance. She glided daintily from the tree to alight on my knee, right next to her counterpart.

"What she is trying to say," this new fairy explained, in a voice so like my other grandmother's, "is that along with the joy of the blessings that you children were, there was also a very deep sorrow that enveloped the entire family. I know that you know what I'm getting at, and, that as an adult you can fully understand, but the child that you were could not, and she became lost in the shuffle. You were only five when your father was taken from you, and when your Mom-mom lost her son."

She gently placed a wing on my Mom-mom's shoulder, and then she continued. "I know that losing your dad at such a young age was traumatic for you. I can see and feel the sadness that is still with you today because of it. But you were too little to understand just how devastating his death was to all of us who shared in his life. That he was no longer with us was excruciating. He was so deeply loved and so sorely missed. We were there, honey, as much as we could be. And as much as you needed us, we needed you more. Just holding one of you in our arms could momentarily ease some of the pain. You were, indeed, our medicine."

"So you see, dear, our lives were a lot more complicated." It was Mom-mom again. "As I mentioned earlier, you were my fourth grandchild and your father's second daughter in as many years. Two more siblings entered your life and ours, so that by the time he was taken from us, he left four babies behind under the age of six. It broke our hearts every time we looked at you, knowing that you would have to grow up without him."

"And there were a lot of you," interjected Grandma. "Can you imagine having four of her at one time?" she exclaimed, laying her miniature hand on Jessi's forehead. There was not a lot of individual attention to go around, but we did our best."

"And we didn't drive," lamented Mom-mom. "We had to depend on our men folk to bring us to see you. Unfortunately, your grandfather could not come to grips with losing your father. When your dear mother brought you to visit, he would put on a happy face for your benefit, but after you left, he would cry his heart out. Because he was raised with the belief that men

46

don't cry, it was easier on his manhood to just not come around so much. That's why I was not able to see you as much as I would have liked to."

"So you see, honey," said Grandma, "the connection to us that you have been longing for all this time has always been there. You just were not able to see it from our perspective, so we came to enlighten you and to erase any doubt."

I was stunned. I could not believe what I was hearing—and seeing. The thought that my grandmothers cared enough about me that they would come to me spiritually was mind-boggling. The tears were flowing freely as the impact of their powerful message began to filter through. I could actually feel a change taking place inside me, like a caterpillar shucking its cocoon and blossoming into a butterfly. My inner child was no longer confused. Thanks to the liberating tidings of comfort from my Sugarplum Grandmothers, she was now set free, able to move forward and mesh with the adult, transforming me into a more serene, secure, and content human being.

My little visitors were both smiling up at me with tears glistening in their eyes. They had succeeded in their mission, and I knew that our precious time together was coming to an end. No words were needed; we were connected, all three of us. We were one in heart, mind and spirit. They fluttered their wings, flew first to kiss Jessi's cheeks, and then my own, and then with a *poof*, and a puff of fairy dust, they were back on the tree.

***

I blink my eyes, and the memory fades.

It is, again, 2008. My granddaughter will be calling shortly to give her final telephone performance before her big day tomorrow. An idea pops into my head, and as I hasten to prepare, I quickly light the candles on the mantle and flip the switch, bringing the Christmas tree to life. I position my Sugarplum Fairies just right. The phone will be on speaker so that they will be able to share in my exclusive recital. I sit in my rocking chair. The phone rings, and as I answer it, I notice an ever-so-slight movement coming from the direction of the Christmas tree. I look up just in time to catch one of the fairies fluffing her wings and the other one winking at me. If I didn't know better, I would have thought I imagined it.

A Christmas for Johnny

Jerome W. McFadden

*J*ohnny stood on the front porch waiting for his mother, stamping his feet against the cold while watching the fat, soft snowflakes fall quietly from the night sky.

The girls were inside, having their nightly argument over who was going to wash and who was going to dry the dishes. He would probably have to go in to settle it, then push them upstairs to brush their teeth and wash their faces and change into their pajamas so they would be ready for bed by the time Mom got home. Their mother would then kiss them, make them say their prayers, and put them to bed. Then she would come downstairs to make everyone's lunch for tomorrow and to prepare tomorrow night's dinner for Johnny to warm up in the microwave and serve. And they would do this all over again.

He saw her walking along the street, more slowly than usual. The strain from working the early shift in the plant, then waiting tables at Bernucci's until they closed, showed on her face.

She gave Johnny a dog-tired smile as she came up the steps and said, "Done your homework?"

"Bad day, Mom?"

She leaned against the porch railing to rest and sighed. She glanced out at the snow that was layering the neighborhood with a quiet blanket of white. The thin scarf that covered her brown hair and the shoulders of her thin grey coat were powdered with

49

snow. "The girls ready for bed?"

"Getting there," Johnny said with a laugh, hoping to share an inside joke with his mother. But she didn't smile at the joke. She gazed into the windows and watched the two girls in the brightly-lit kitchen.

Johnny didn't bother to look around. "What's wrong, Mom?"

She snapped open her purse and took out a ten dollar bill and said morosely, "This is all I have. Rent was due today. I expected a Christmas bonus from the plant, but Mr. Aronson said I had not been with the company long enough for a Christmas bonus. This is all there was for tips tonight. Nobody was eating out this close to Christmas."

Johnny looked at the tenner but didn't take it, not knowing what his mother wanted

"Take it, Johnny, and then tomorrow go to Stinson's and find some gifts for your sisters, as best you can. They need something for Christmas."

Johnny nodded. He would find whatever ten dollars would buy. They would each have a present for Christmas the day after tomorrow.

His mother gave him a sad smile. "I'll buy you a nice present on your birthday in February. But they are just little girls, and you are a big boy. They need to have a Christmas. They're so used to doing without. They need a Christmas. You are the man of the house. You understand, don't you?"

She kissed him on the forehead and went on into the house, finding the energy to tease the girls about not being ready for bed. Johnny followed her into the house, already making plans for the following day.

It was cold and blustery the next morning when Johnny set out for the store. It was the day before Christmas, and there was no school. His mother had already left for work, so he had fed the girls, then arranged for Mrs. Watkins to watch them while he was gone. He walked the eight blocks to Stinson's, thinking desperately about how to get the most for his ten dollars.

The streets were decorated with small Christmas trees attached to the street lights, and shiny gold bunting hung across the road. The snow had continued to fall all night and the neighborhood was white and clean and cheerful.

An elderly couple was walking along, smiling, holding hands. They said, "Merry Christmas!" as they passed Johnny.

Johnny mumbled, "Merry Christmas," in return, but his voice sounded discouraged, even to him. It was hard to be this poor when everyone else seemed to be so happy.

He saw a Christmas tree lot across the street from Stinson's. A few people were picking through the remaining trees while others strapped them to the tops of their cars. Everyone seemed impatient to get home to put the trees up before Christmas Eve.

Johnny crossed the street, just to look. The smell of fresh pine was delightful. There was one tree in front of the lot, being used as a sample tree, all decorated and already lit up even though it was just late morning. Johnny stopped to admire it, wishing it were his.

"Need a tree, son?"

Johnny turned to see a bearded older man standing behind him. He wore a Mackinaw coat and plaid hat with flaps to protect his ears against the cold.

"Just looking," Johnny said, then turned to walk across the street to Stinson's. But halfway across, he stopped and turned back to the man, stunned by his own boldness. "How much do you want for that tree, sir?"

"Five dollars."

"Including the decorations?"

"No, son. They are not for sale. Just the tree. I use the same decorations every year."

"I'll give you two bucks for the tree, with the decorations."

The man laughed and then said, "You can have the tree for two bucks as it has a little wear and tear from being out front for the past three weeks, but you have to take the decorations down and put them into the box over there."

"Two bucks, with the decorations," Johnny persisted.

"Two bucks without the decorations," the man repeated.

Johnny smiled, forcing himself not to back off. "Those decorations are looking a little tattered."

The man looked at Johnny long and hard. His cheeks were red from the cold. His eyes were a deep blue and seemed as cold as the wind that was ruffling through the trees. He then looked over at the tree and said, "They are looking a little tattered. I should probably put up some new ones next year. But I tell you what, you come back here the day after Christmas and help me clean up and you can have the tree and decorations for a buck and half."

"Two bucks if you let me have the stand, too."

The man laughed. "Damn, son, you drive a hard bargain. I like that. But you'd better be here at eight o'clock the day after Christmas."

"I'll be here at eight. And I'll work all day. I promise."

The man gave Johnny a box and a small ladder so he could reach the decorations and said, "Go to it, son."

Johnny carefully took the bulbs off the tree and packed them into the box. He unwound the one straggly string of lights, but had to tip the tree on its side to pull off the small silver angel that crowned the top.

Then he faced the problem of getting the five-foot tree and the box of decorations home, but he decided to solve that after he finished his shopping at Stinson's across the street. The man agreed to guard the tree and box while Johnny ran over to the store, yelling after him with a laugh, "You gonna bargain with them, too?"

After being outside for so long, the warmth of the store felt good. Christmas carols were playing in the background. Johnny suddenly felt relief washing over him, as if he were starting to believe that this might turn into a good Christmas after all.

He went through the aisles and grabbed a Monopoly game for the family to share, a box of sixty-four Crayola crayons and three coloring books for Cindy, and a small, stuffed Raggedy Ann doll for Kathy. All of the checkout counters were closed except one. Johnny recognized Mrs. Stinson from previous visits and was surprised to see her working as a cashier. Johnny put his merchandise on the counter, behind another customer, and waited.

Mrs. Stinson smiled when it became Johnny's turn. "You're the last customer. We're closing up at noon."

Johnny pulled out his remaining eight dollars and put them on the counter.

Mrs. Stinson looked down at the eight dollars, frowning. "You're little short. This all comes to sixteen thirty-three."

Johnny opened his mouth but the words wouldn't come out. He stared down at his feet, crestfallen. He should have looked closer at the price tags.

"You want to take some of it back?" Mrs. Stinson gently asked.

"No," Johnny said in a whisper.

"We don't do lay-aways. Not on dolls and crayons."

Johnny hesitated and then said, "Could I work it off?"

"Work it off?" Mrs. Stinson said, dumbfounded.

"You know," Johnny said, "come in and help you around the store. Take down the Christmas decorations, sweep the floor, whatever? School is out for two weeks. I'll come in for however many days you want."

Mrs. Stinson glanced at her watch as if anxious to close down and get out of the store. "I've seen you in here before, haven't I?"

"We live just down the street. My mom comes in all the time, with my two sisters. For Tide soap and toilet paper and other things. Me, too."

Mrs. Stinson sighed and then said, "Okay, it's a deal. You come in here the day after Christmas and see me, first thing in the morning."

Johnny hesitated before saying, "I'm sorry, Mrs. Stinson. I can't. I have promised to work across the street in the Christmas tree lot that day. To pay off a Christmas tree. But I can be in here bright and early on December twenty-seventh."

Mrs. Stinson gave Johnny a wide smile. "I see. Okay, we can do that. Do you want your Christmas presents wrapped?"

Johnny looked at the woman in disbelief, not able to hide his smile. "Yes. Please."

After Mrs. Stinson finished the wrapping, Johnny carried the presents back across the street to the tree lot and placed them in the big box with the decorations and tree stand. He then began the long trudge home, dragging the tree a few yards along the snow filled sidewalk, then stopping to retrieve the big box, and the repeating the process over and over. It was tedious. He was sweating in spite of the cold, and the eight blocks looked very long.

Then he heard a car stop and a voice say, "You need some help, Johnny?"

He looked over to see Mrs. Stinson behind the wheel.

"Thanks, Mrs. Stinson, but I don't want to bother you."

"It's not a bother, Johnny. I'm going in that direction anyway."

Johnny shrugged to indicate that he would accept Mrs. Stinson's help if she was really sincere about it.

They put the box in the back seat and opened the car trunk to jam in the tree. It wouldn't close, but they fastened it with some string that Mrs. Stinson had in the glove compartment. The eight blocks then became a two-minute drive instead of an hour-long walk.

They unloaded the tree and the box in front of the house, and Johnny wished Mrs. Stinson a merry Christmas, saying that he would see her on December twenty-seventh, bright and early. He then carted everything up the steps, onto the porch, and then into the house.

Cindy and Kathy squealed with delight and amazement when they saw the tree, and then quickly helped him pull everything through the door. He put them to work setting up the tree and stringing the decorations and hanging the bulbs, shooing them away from the presents, saying they had to wait for Mom to come home before they could open anything.

His mother was stunned when she walked into the house that evening. "How did you . . ."

"I'll tell you later," Johnny said. "It's beautiful, isn't it?"

"And the presents?"

"I'll explain later."

His mother started crying and crossed the room to hug him, kissing him on the forehead and on the cheek. "This is so wonderful."

They made some popcorn and the four of them crowded together on the sofa to admire their tree with the silver angel on top and their presents lying beneath it. They turned on the television and watched *It's A Wonderful Life.* Before bed, they tore open the three wrapped presents. The girls oooed and ahhhhed over the doll and the big box of crayons, and then immediately wanted to play the Monopoly game, but Mother said, "No, everyone to bed. We will play the game in the morning, after we come back from Mass."

The three of them went up the stairs, sounding happy and excited about Christmas. Johnny sat quietly on the sofa smiling at the tree and the silver angel, happy to feel that maybe he was becoming the man of the house.

Mis-conceptions

Courtney Annicchiarico

"*G*reg." I took a deep breath failing to suppress my smile. "I think I'm pregnant."

"Really?" Greg squeaked, his eyes wide with surprise. "That's great! Why 'think?' Did you take a test?" He was half way out of his chair before I stopped him with a raised hand.

I poked at my omelet to stall for a second. "Well . . . that's the thing. I've taken two, and they're both negative." Greg's goofy smile drooped and he arched his brow. "But," I hurried on, "I felt cramps a few weeks ago and I spotted a little and Alison said those could be signs of very early pregnancy." He looked skeptical. "Alison's a nurse, Greg."

"So," he drew out the word a little, trying to keep up. "Alison thinks you're pregnant?"

"Well . . . no. No she doesn't, because of the tests. But I think I am."

"Hmmm. Well, we'll see, right?" Greg said, clearly deflated.

"You don't believe me," I said more than asked. I got up and cleared the table.

"I believe," Greg said, choosing his words carefully, no doubt watching as his barely touched breakfast was scraped down the disposal, "you want to have a baby and you're very excited to get pregnant. I am, too."

"And you don't believe me," I accused. Greg stood up and walked over to stand by me at the sink.

He looked away from me and focused on the wall. After a moment, he turned back. "I think you may be psyching yourself up. How pregnant do you think you are?"

I cringed because I knew this would do nothing for my credibility. "Two weeks plus a few days."

Greg laughed and wrapped his arms around me. "You've taken two tests already? Honey, have you even missed your period?" I lightly punched his side. He knows how much I hate that condescending tone.

"Yesterday," I grumbled against his chest. Maybe I was being childish, getting all excited when there was no reason. "And . . . it's really three tests." I rolled my eyes and paused before continuing. "I went to my doctor. That one was negative, too."

"Well," Greg said, tipping my head up, "we'll see, right?"

***

Two weeks later, Greg and I were making dinner.

"Ummmm, Greg?" I started nervously.

"Yeah?"

"I'm two weeks late now, and . . ."

"That's not unusual for you," he interrupted in a slightly sing song way that made me want to punch him.

"*And* . . ." I continued, no longer nervous. "I've been getting nauseous."

Greg stopped chopping carrots and wrapped his arms around me. "It's the end of cold and flu season," he said. "You're a teacher, and three quarters of your students are probably sick. Wait to see if you get sick, too."

He's lucky I didn't claw his face.

"I don't know. I don't feel like I've got a cold or flu,"

I said. Something in my tone must have sounded hopeful because he eyed me suspiciously.

"You want to go to the doctor again, don't you?"

I mumbled something I knew he couldn't have heard, but he guessed correctly.

"Court-ney!"

"Gre-eg!" I mimicked, stretching his name to two syllables. "It was negative, if you want to know."

"I figured."

"But," I said, trying to win him over, "I peeked at the chart on the doctor's wall. I'll be due December second, if we're pregnant." I thought using "we" was a nice touch. "It could be a great Christmas," I joked.

"I don't know why you're so convinced the tests are wrong." I could tell by the way his eyes tightened that he was getting agitated.

"Why are you so eager to believe the tests are right?"

"That's not fair!" He was back to chopping with such vigor that I was mildly concerned he was going to cut his finger. "I just don't want to be disappointed," he continued. "Four tests can't be wrong."

"Greg . . . I keep getting queasy during my last class of the day. If I were sick, would it happen the same time every day?"

"Would it happen that way if you were pregnant?" Greg said in an argumentative tone that matched my own.

"I don't know. I've never been pregnant before, but I *have* been sick, and I *know* it doesn't work that way when I'm sick. I'm telling you, I don't care what the tests say. I'm pregnant." I looked back to the lettuce.

He took a deep breath. "Court, you're just thinking so much about it that your body is having the most common symptoms. It's a normal reaction."

"Really, Greg?" I squared my shoulders and glared

at him. "You know this from your vast experience with a uterus?"

"I can't talk to you when you get like this." Greg threw up his hands and stormed out of the room.

"And what *way* would that be, Greg? *Correct?*" I yelled after him. I was pretty sure he heard me before the door closed.

***

"Shouldn't you have your period, though?" Greg asked later that night while we were in bed. His tone was soft. It was the first time we had spoken in five hours.

"My doctor's not too worried," I answered.

"But . . ." Greg ventured, trying again to appease me, "doesn't it make planning a pregnancy harder?"

"Guess so." *You're so not getting off this easy!* I thought.

"Well . . . I don't want to wait. I guess I'm getting impatient, because I want to have a baby with you."

I turned over in bed and smiled at him. He beamed back.

"Good luck with that." I smirked as I rolled back over and turned off the light.

***

A week passed and I refused to talk to Greg about how I was feeling day to day. *Maybe he's right,* I thought more and more.

***

"Greg?" I asked when he picked up on the second ring. "Do you think you can come home early?"

"Why?" he whispered. His voice sounded concerned.

I didn't often ask him to come home early from work.

"I think I'm going to go back to my doctor." I scanned the teachers' lounge to make sure I wasn't overheard. I hadn't confided in any of my friends at work yet.

Greg sighed into the phone. "Court, didn't you take a home test a few days ago?"

"Yes." I swallowed to clear my throat. I had been weepy for a few days, but I was trying to hide that from Greg. He would interpret the mood swings as PMS, and I didn't, so why argue? "But listen, okay?" I said to fill the silence. "I couldn't drink my coffee this morning." I didn't think he understood the magnitude of my revelation, so I went on. "Really, one sip and I was running to the bathroom." Still nothing. "That's weird for me, Greg. And stranger yet, I didn't want it after I got back to my seat in the lounge. The thought of it made me more queasy so I ended up throwing it away."

"You can still be getting sick," Greg said, but there was a little bit of a question lurking under the statement.

"I'd have coffee pumped through an IV if I were sick." I laughed.

"Hmm. That's true."

He's starting to believe me, I thought. "And there's more. The school went to church today for Holy Thursday. I actually just got back. I was on my way up to receive Communion and I suddenly thought to myself, *I really want crunchy cheese doodles*! Greg . . . that's just not normal."

He snorted into the phone. "No, I guess it isn't."

"Do you think you can leave a little early? Just be home by five o'clock? I'll be back from the doctor by then."

"I'll do my best. Cutting out forty-five minutes early shouldn't be a problem."

"Okay," I chirped. I didn't want to get too excited,

and I really didn't want to get Greg's hopes up.

"And, Court?"

"Yeah?"

"Good luck." He sounded like he was ten years old. "I love you."

"Me, too." Then I hung up, called my doctor for an appointment, and went to finish my day. I was blushing like a fool.

***

I was sitting in a paper gown by three thirty. For the third time in less than a month, I peed in a cup and waited. I heard a soft knock on the door and I knew as soon as I saw my doctor's face that the result was negative.

"Do another test," I said. I explained what had happened with the coffee that morning but her face remained unreadable. "Coffee is second only to oxygen for me. I just don't function without it." I sighed. She wasn't getting it. "Please, do another test."

"Okay." I took a deep breath and my doctor continued. "I can do a blood test. I don't think you're pregnant, but," she said with a sigh, "I can't explain why you're five weeks late." I nodded and smiled weakly. I hated needles but I was relieved I'd finally get a positive result. She smiled and left to get a nurse.

It wasn't so bad. Just one vial to fill. The doctor came back in when it was over and handed me a prescription. "I'll get the result of the blood test in a few days. If it's negative, that means you're not pregnant." She paused so I could digest that fact. "I know you and Greg want to start a family. Fill this." She nodded to the square paper in my hand. "The pills will jump-start your cycle and get you back on track." She patted my knee and squeezed my shoulder before she left.

***

I went home and waited. Three days later, the doctor called and told me it was safe to take the pills. I appreciated that she put that positive spin on the news, but I still blurted out, "It's negative?" She said it was, and my knees wobbled. I hung up the phone and called Greg. I wasn't pregnant. Absolutely.

I drove to CVS to fill the prescription. I had the paper, complete with the doctor's illegible signature, in my hand, but I couldn't do it. After forty minutes of pacing, I bought three magazines, two lipsticks, and razor blades for Greg just so I didn't look like a pharmacy stalker. I prepared myself for the argument that was sure to occur when Greg got home that night. I cried, because I knew he'd be furious. Clearly and understandably, he would want me to trust my doctor and move forward. Wasn't I being illogical? How many tests did I need to spell it out? But starting up my cycle would mean I would lose the baby no one but me believed was there. But did I believe it, or was I just being stubborn and neurotic? As I walked back to my car, my hand rested on my stomach. I cursed at how stupid the gesture was.

***

Greg was beaming when he walked through the door. He shrugged off his coat and hung it over a kitchen chair before he plopped down next to me on our couch. He cocked his head to one side and looked at me for a long while. "Don't take the pills," he said in a nonchalant voice. A hearty laugh preceded my sob of relief. Greg wasn't giving me advice. He was giving me the answer to all my questions and ending my deliberations. "Okay?" He laughed as I tackled him and started peppering his cheeks with kisses.

"Okay." I sniffed. "You're not mad?"

Greg looked at me, his eyes glistening with tears that he quickly wiped away. "No. You have to trust yourself."

"You don't think I'm being silly?" I asked.

"Oh, I think you're silly!" he chided, buckling over to protect his abdomen from my elbow. "But I also think you just may be pregnant."

***

I was back in the waiting room less than two weeks later. I was exhausted and I couldn't turn my head without my stomach rebelling. I had asked Greg to take me to the hospital but he insisted on taking me to my doctor first.

"I really think I'm seriously sick," I moaned. "I must be."

"Maybe you have morning sickness?"

"Impossible. Nothing could feel this bad and not require urgent medical attention."

"Just humor me," Greg said, patting my arm. "After this, I'll take you anywhere you want to go."

A nurse entered the waiting area and told me to follow her. Once again, I was in an all-too-familiar bathroom and given yet another cup. This time I did what I needed to do with no hope or expectations. I walked into the examination room where Greg was waiting, and whimpered as I stepped up onto the bed. Greg sat on a stool against the wall and tried to comfort me. When the doctor came in, I barely looked up, but I did notice a small stack of magazines she carried under my chart. *What are those for?* I thought. Then I saw a yellow Post-it stuck to the first page of my file. It said just one word: yes.

Greg saw it, too. We just had time to look at each other before my doctor shouted, "Congratulations,

Mom and Dad!"

Greg whooped and popped up from his perch. He bounced off the wall behind him, crashed into the counter at his side, and then hit the wall again. When he was finally still, it was only for a second. He bounded to my side with as little grace but all the enthusiasm of a puppy that has no idea how big its paws are.

"You're pregnant! You're really pregnant!"

***

I went for an ultrasound a few days later, and the technician confirmed what I had known. I was over seven weeks along. My little Noah had been with me the whole time. And it was, in fact, a great Christmas.

You Better Watch Out
Carol L. Wright

"Great party, Joy," Wendell Owens said, taking a snowball cookie from the tray. "It just wouldn't be the Christmas season without your open house."

"Thanks, Wendell." Joy smiled at her guest. "For a while there, I wasn't sure I'd be able to put an open house together this year. I've been so busy at work."

"That would have been our loss," Wendell said. "Where would we all go after lighting the town Christmas tree?"

Wendell was a jovial man, who, when suited up in red fur and supplied with a white beard, made a very convincing Santa Claus for the town tree lighting every first Friday of December. As a long-time resident, and publisher and editor of the New England village's weekly newspaper, he knew every child in town by name. When he handed out gifts at the town celebration, he always had a comment or two that made each child wonder how Santa really knew whether they had been bad or good that year.

"Well, I'm glad to help keep the town's disreputable characters off the streets." Joy laughed as she looked around at the members of the Board of Selectmen, the minister from the Congregational Church, the town's only doctor, and several of Joy's colleagues from her law practice who filled her living room. The church organist regaled the group with variations of songs of the season on Joy's upright piano.

The doorbell rang, barely audible over the laughter and music.

Joy shook her head. "Don't they know it's an *open* house?" she said and handed her tray to her teenage daughter, Holly. "Take care of this for me, will you, sweetie?"

By the time Joy reached the front door, her husband, Nick, was already opening it. She could see the blue and black of the police officer's uniform and the reflection of his leather holster in the porch light.

"What's happened?" she asked, before Nick or the officer could speak.

"Accident," Officer Dan Davis said. "Dr. Barnes here?"

"Is someone hurt?"

"I got a call. Jimmy Kerrigan fell off his roof a few blocks down. He's in a bad way. His sister called for an ambulance. Figured since I was nearby I'd get Dr. Barnes if he's here."

"I'll get him," Joy said, turning toward her guests. She had no trouble picking out Dr. Barnes. He was tall and thin, about forty, with a pock-marked face that looked like it never held a smile. He had just moved to town from Springfield to open a small practice and to take a job as a part-time medical examiner. People were glad to finally have a doctor in the community, but his permanently dour expression held friendly overtures at bay. Joy approached him, but had to call his name before he noticed her.

"Dr. Barnes, there's a police officer at the door."

The doctor flinched. "Why tell me?"

"They need you immediately. There's been an accident."

"Dead people aren't usually in much of a hurry," Dr. Barnes said with a scowl, "so this one must still be alive."

"Yes, and in need of medical attention. Please hurry." Joy took Barnes by the arm and led him to the door. "Do you have your medical bag?"

"In my car," Barnes said as he grabbed the coat Nick handed to him and left with the officer.

"Oh dear," Joy said to Nick as he closed the door. "I hope everything is all right. I feel like going over to see if there's anything I can do to help."

"You can't help the doctor, Joy. And you don't want to appear to be an ambulance chaser," Nick said with a wink.

Joy grimaced. "I guess you're right."

"Thanks for a wonderful time," Wendell said as he rushed past Joy and Nick to follow the police, putting his coat on as he went. The life of a newspaperman was always subject to interruption.

"Now *he's* an ambulance chaser." Joy and Nick laughed after closing the door.

***

Once the party was over and the dishes done, Joy's thoughts turned to Jimmy Kerrigan. He was a life-long resident of the small town, and had run a local auto repair shop for several decades before selling it and retiring. Since then, he kept busy as a handy-man. Joy guessed he must be in his late seventies. He and his sister, Margaret, lived in the modest house where they grew up. Like his sister, Jimmy had never married. He was one of those local institutions whom everyone recognized and thought well of, but who never seemed to be part of any of the goings-on in town. An independent New Englander. Joy hoped his independent spirit would help him recover from his fall.

It was after one in the morning, and Joy couldn't sleep. Nick snored in the bed next to her, but she got up and walked into the hallway. She crept past Holly's room, across the hall to the spare bedroom that they used as a library, to look for a book to help her get to sleep. Once there, she decided to call the police department non-emergency number to see if she could get an update on Jimmy Kerrigan's condition.

"Well, you didn't hear it from me," the dispatcher told Joy, "but I hear he has some broken bones and he's in a coma."

"Do they know why he was on the roof?" Joy asked.

"His sister said he was trying to fix a skylight before that snow moves in tonight."

"In the dark? That doesn't seem like a very good idea, does it?"

"Turned out not to be."

New England understatement.

***

By morning, the ground was covered with eight inches of new snow. Shortly after dawn, Nick was outside clearing their driveway and the sidewalk in front of their century-old house. Joy started the coffee maker and prepared milk and eggs so she could make French toast as soon as he came inside. She didn't expect to see Holly up for at least a while.

Joy settled down with the morning's *Springfield Republican*. There was a story about a man from Longmeadow who went to court to keep from having to tear down his stone wall, one about a Connecticut teen who robbed an old woman and was tracked all the way to Amherst, and a report on Christmas illustrations at the Norman Rockwell museum in Stockbridge. Nothing, of course, about Jimmy Kerrigan. She knew that Wendell Owens would cover the story in the *Town Monitor*, but it wasn't due out for another five days. She thought about calling the police station again to find out what was going on. Instead, she started heating the griddle, and set the kettle to boil for a cup of tea.

Before the teakettle whistled, Nick came onto the covered porch by the kitchen door, stomping snow off his boots. Joy poured a cup of coffee, and handed it to him as soon as he had his coat off.

"Thanks, hon." Nick smiled, removing his fogged-over sunglasses. "It's a nice packing snow out there." Nick's cheeks were bright red, and Joy could see a sparkle in his hazel eyes. It wasn't the first snow of the season, but so far it was the biggest. It seemed to have put Nick in the holiday mood.

"Maybe I can get Holly to build a snowman with me after she gets up." Nick's grin showed off his dimples. They always made Joy smile.

"I have two kids," Joy said, ruffling Nick's hair.

After breakfast was cleared away, something about the sun reflecting on the new snow drew Joy outside.

"I think I'll take a walk, Nick," she said.

"Sure thing. Hey, if you're in town, could you pick up some bread? It looks like the French toast nearly wiped us out."

"Sure." Joy bundled up for the six-block walk. While some of the sidewalks were not yet cleared, the roads were cleaned down to wet pavement. An occasional car spit slush up along the curb, but Joy was quick enough to avoid being splashed.

Turning a corner, she saw the proud blue spruce that always served as the town Christmas tree, glistening with new-fallen snow. Joy thought about the legend of Martin Luther seeing a snow-covered evergreen during an evening walk in the woods. It glowed in the moonlight, and left the religious reformer so awestruck that he brought a tree home and lit it with

71

candles to share it with his family. Joy could understand his wonder when nature decorates itself so well.

She ducked into the local grocer's and picked up a loaf of bread. Walking along the town green, Joy smiled at the children shouting at each other from behind snow forts. Then she glanced into the windows of the various merchants, each with a new holiday display. When she came to the office of the *Town Monitor*, she peered in the front window, hoping to see Wendell inside. The office was dark.

"Casing the joint?"

Joy jumped at the voice behind her. Turning, she saw Wendell carrying a box of doughnuts and a tall paper cup of coffee.

"Wendell! No—I was just wondering if you were inside."

"Nope, but if you'll wait a second, I will be." He pulled out his key and opened the door. Joy followed. The office smelled of stale coffee, dust, and old paper. He put the box of doughnuts down, and lifted the lid to offer one to Joy. She surveyed the array, all frosted and decorated with holiday sprinkles.

"Uh, no thanks."

"So," Wendell said, taking a bite of a chocolate frosted, "what brings you to my office?"

"I was just wondering what happened last night with Jimmy Kerrigan."

"Oh. Tough old buzzard, Jimmy. We got there before the ambulance. Dr. Barnes looked at him, and then the EMTs arrived and took him off to county hospital. I got some pictures for this week's paper." Wendell pulled a digital camera out of a desk drawer and turned it on. "Here's where last night's pictures start."

Joy looked at the camera's display and saw a photo of Jimmy Kerrigan, lying on the ground, his face contorted in pain.

"He was conscious when you got there?" Joy asked.

"Yeah. He was mumbling something, but I couldn't make it out. Poor old guy."

Joy pushed a button, and the picture dissolved, revealing another.

"What is Dr. Barnes doing?" Joy showed the newspaperman a photo of Dr. Barnes, with his face turned to the side, hovering over the injured man's head.

"Don't know. Listening for a heartbeat?"

Joy shook her head. "That's not his chest. Maybe trying to see if he's breathing?"

"That doesn't make sense. He was conscious."

"True. What did Dr. Barnes do for him?" Joy asked, handing the camera back to Wendell.

"Nothing much. The EMTs were there a moment after we got to the scene. They took over, and Barnes didn't even go in the ambulance. I guess the cops didn't need him after all. It worked out for me, though. I don't know how long it would have been before I heard about this if they hadn't come by your house to collect Dr. Barnes. And I wouldn't have gotten these pictures."

"What do you hear from the hospital?"

"Nothing. The hospital won't answer questions from the press due to patient privacy laws, and his sister isn't answering the phone. You know these old New Englanders. Their business is their business—not yours."

"Well, it's Saturday. Here's hoping that by Thursday, you have some good news to report in the paper."

"It'll have to come by Tuesday at four. That's when I have to send the paper to press."

"I hope he'll come around by then." Something about the accident had put a damper on Joy's holiday spirit that even the splendor of the town Christmas tree could not repair. Perhaps it was the way it had interrupted her holiday open house; maybe it was just because Jimmy Kerrigan was such a town institution. She shook her head as she walked home, the loaf of bread swinging at her side.

When she got home, she smiled at a small snowman standing in the yard. Inside, she found Nick

in the library grading papers. He taught history at the county community college, and as the end of the semester approached, the term papers flowed in.

"I don't know why you assign so much work for your students," Joy teased him. "If you didn't assign it, you wouldn't have to grade it."

"And they would know no more at the end of the class than they did at the beginning." Nick grimaced and removed his reading glasses. "Although, from the look of these papers, I'm not sure how much they've learned."

"Poor baby," Joy cooed, rubbing Nick's shoulders. "That's a cute snowman outside. Where's Holly?"

"She went over to Bethany's house to work on some project for school."

"Great. How about I make us some lunch?"

***

After lunch, Nick took his iPod and returned to the library and his grading. Joy settled down at the dining room table with her address book and a couple of boxes of Christmas cards. It was the first weekend of December, but Joy knew that getting their cards out was a long process. She always tried to write a personal note in each one, and she had a feeling that would be hard for her to do that year. To help put her in the Christmas spirit, she put on some Christmas music, lit a fire in the living room fireplace, and made herself a cup of holiday blend tea. Before long, she was humming along with "I'll Be Home for Christmas," and admiring her growing stack of completed cards.

That close to the winter solstice, the sun set early. By five o'clock it was fully dark outside, and Holly still had not returned from her friend's house. Joy texted her daughter's cell with a message that dinner would be at six. Then, she went to work preparing the meal.

With water running and pans rattling, Joy didn't notice any noises coming from outside. She flipped on the backyard light and smiled through the kitchen window at the bird tracks in the snow under the birdfeeder. Nick kept it filled all winter long. Just then, a load of snow fell from the roof, dropping past the window. Joy was surprised that there was enough melting after dark to loosen the snow. Maybe they needed more attic insulation.

A pot of spaghetti sauce simmered on the stove as Joy prepared cutlets for chicken parmesan. The windows steamed up as she boiled pasta. Cooking usually put Joy in a good mood, but the image of poor Jimmy Kerrigan, lying injured on the ground with Dr. Barnes hovering over him, was something she couldn't shake.

Just as she was about to drain the pasta, she sensed a presence behind her. She dropped the pot into the sink, and whirled around to find Nick leaning in for a hug.

"You scared me half to death."

"What? I was just coming in to see if I could help with dinner."

"I could have scalded us both. Never sneak up on a woman cooking pasta."

"I'll make a note of that. So, do you want me to make the salad?"

"Sure. I'll try to salvage the spaghetti. Is Holly home yet?"

"Haven't seen her; I've been upstairs grading."

"What could be taking her so long? Perhaps we should call Bethany's house and see if she has left yet."

"Ahhhhhhhhhhhh!"

At the sound of a scream outside, Joy and Nick raced to the front door. Nick pulled it open to see Holly standing halfway up the front walk, clearly panicked, but apparently uninjured.

"What happened? Are you okay?" Nick yelled as he ran to his daughter.

"Ohmigod, Dad, are *you* okay? I thought I just saw you fall off of our roof!"

Joy followed Holly's frightened gaze. Outlined in the snow was the figure of a man dressed in red fur with white trim.

"Nick, call 9-1-1," Joy said, dashing over to the prone figure. "Wendell? Wendell! Are you all right? We're calling an ambulance. You're going to be fine." She touched the man's neck and felt for a pulse. She could not find any. She lifted the man's shoulder and tried to turn him onto his back so that she could start CPR.

"Uh, Mom, that's not Mr. Owens," Holly said, coming up behind her.

"What?" Joy asked, looking for the first time at the man's face. "Who is it?"

"I guess it's Santa."

***

Once the EMTs arrived, Joy took Holly inside to warm her up, and make sure she was no worse off for the shock she had received. Next, she called Wendell. She knew it was not he who had fallen on her lawn, but she needed to hear his voice to be reassured that he was all right.

"Weekly Monitor," Wendell answered the phone on the first ring.

"Wendell. It's Joy. There's been another accident, only this time it was at our house."

"Your house? Is anyone hurt? What happened?"

Joy took the phone to the window and watched as the police taped off the scene and the crime scene unit arrived.

"We're okay, but someone has . . ." she had trouble saying the word. "I think someone has died."

"I'll be right over."

***

The next morning, the doorbell rang as Joy, Nick, and Holly were getting ready for church. Nick opened the door to Officer Dan Davis.

"Dan. Come in. Don't you even get Sundays off?"

"Not when there's been an unexplained death in town. And right after Jimmy Kerrigan's accident, too." He shook his head. "Why do people think it's a good idea to be up on a roof in the middle of winter?"

"Do you have any information on who that guy was, or why he was here?" Joy asked, joining the men in the living room.

"Yeah. I thought you folks would like to know. He didn't have any ID on him, but we ran his prints. He has a lot of aliases, but the name he uses most is Harry Watts. Does that ring a bell with either of you?"

Nick and Joy looked at each other, and shook their heads.

"He's a second-story man with a long rap sheet. I guess he decided to bring his business to town. Too bad he picked the night after a big snowstorm. You can see on your roof how he slid on the snow. Half of your roof is wiped bare."

Joy remembered seeing snow fall past the kitchen window.

"A burglar? Here?" Nick said. "We haven't had any real crime in town as long as I have lived here. That's one of the reasons we like it. It's far enough away from the city to avoid their problems."

"Well, this guy's last known address was in Springfield. But city folk have cars, too. No one is safe these days. I wish I could convince more people to lock their doors."

"He came an awfully long way to die." Joy shuddered. "Do you have any idea why he was dressed as Santa Claus?"

"No real theories on that. And we can't ask him."

Nick shook his head. "Is there anything else we can help you with, Dan?"

"Nope. I think I got everything I needed last night. Let me know, though, if you think of anything, or remember ever running into this guy Watts. There will be an autopsy, of course, but I think we'll find that he died of . . . overconfidence."

***

Joy usually found that being at work pushed personal problems to the back of her mind, but the next day, she found it hard to concentrate. It's not every day that a man dies in your yard. She couldn't get the image of him lying in the snow out of her mind. What was he doing there? Why did he come all the way from Springfield to burglarize their house? And why was he dressed as Santa?

On her lunch break, she went over to the newspaper office, to see if Wendell had any more information on either of the two falls.

"From what I've been able to gather, there's no change in Jimmy's condition. The doctors don't know if he'll ever wake up," Wendell told Joy.

80

"How's his sister holding up?" Joy asked.

"Tough old bird. She's okay, and even if she weren't she wouldn't let anybody know it."

"What a terrible Christmas season this is. Do you know any more about this Harry Watts character?"

"My sources in Springfield confirm that he was in and out of jail most of his life. His last stint was for robbing the houses of the recently deceased, while their families were burying them."

"I've heard of that happening. How awful to add such an injury to people who are already burdened with sorrow."

"I don't think that mattered much to him."

"But that really doesn't explain what happened here. Why would he come all the way from Springfield? And why would he dress as Santa?"

"No idea."

"And Nick and I were home. Is it likely he would change his M.O. so dramatically without a reason?"

"Maybe his reason was that he got caught with the old one."

Joy considered this, but it didn't seem to be a sufficient explanation. "No. It has to be something more. Something had to bring him here. And I can assure you it was not our collection of paperback books and refrigerator art. Maybe he has a connection with someone in town. Do you know anyone with connections in Springfield?"

"Well, let's see. Most of the businesses in town probably have contacts there. It's a decent-sized city, after all. Some wholesalers there. I think the bank's regional corporate office is there. Not sure what else."

"I don't think that's it. It has to be more, I don't know. More personal, I guess."

"Oh, you mean like family in Springfield? Sure. Some folks probably have relatives there, or went to school there, or something like that. Hey, I think the Carlton's kid goes to college in Springfield."

Something had been nagging at the back of Joy's brain, but she couldn't bring it into focus. Then, she remembered.

"I've got it. Dr. Barnes is from Springfield."

"True. But a lot of people are from Springfield, Joy. That doesn't mean anything. Just because he's an unpleasant S.O.B. doesn't mean he's in cahoots with a burglar."

"But don't you see how it fits? Dr. Barnes is a medical examiner. Medical examiners know about who has died. He and Watts could have been working to-gether all this time. So when Barnes moved, Watts came, too."

"But no one died at your house, Joy. In fact, no one has died in town all month, except for Watts. This would be a lousy place for him to take up his old habits."

Joy could not come up with a response. She really felt that she was onto something, but the pieces didn't fit. Or perhaps some of the pieces were still missing.

When she got home, she tried her theory on Nick. "Maybe," she said, "he was casing our house during the party, and that's why Watts came here."

"If he were casing our house, it wouldn't take him long to figure out we don't have much of any value," Nick said. "Don't let your imagination run away with you, Joy. Sometimes it's better to just let it go and be glad that Watts didn't harm anyone other than him-self."

It always annoyed Joy when Nick accused her of having an over-active imagination, but she had to ad-mit he had a point.

***

On Wednesday morning, Joy heard the good news. Wendell called her office to tell her that Jimmy Kerrigan had regained consciousness. He was still groggy, and did not remember the fall, but the prognosis was good. The news lifted Joy's spirits.

***

As expected, Thursday's *Town Monitor* had both falls on the front page. "Nightmares on Elm Street" read the somewhat hyperbolic banner headline. Joy was glad that at least one nightmare appeared to be nearing its end.

Wendell had devoted the entire top of the paper to the two accidents and had included photos of each of the victims. Taking up three columns on the left-hand side of the paper was a subhead reading "Local injured on West Elm." Below it was an account of Jimmy Kerrigan's fall. Wendell included comments from neighbors who were not surprised Jimmy tried to do the repairs himself. "He never met a job he didn't think he could handle," one friend was quoted as saying. "His work is always first rate," said another. A former customer of his garage said he was honest. There was even a quotation from someone who had known him since high school that mentioned his impish sense of humor. Reading it, Joy wished she had known him better. Jimmy's photo, located next to the subhead, looked like it was taken about thirty years ago. *Wendell probably got it from his sister,* thought Joy.

Of more interest to her, however, was the right hand side of the page where two columns in a shaded box held a subhead reading "Suspect dies in fall on East Elm." The picture, located near the fold, seemed to be an old mug shot of Harry Watts. She looked at the photo, trying to see if she could discern anything familiar, but had no success. She scanned the article, mostly drawn, it appeared, from the archives of the *Springfield Republican,* with information on his last crime from Officer Dan Davis. Joy had not thought until that moment how nice it was that Wendell had not sought a comment from her, or worse from Holly, about the incident. Nothing in the article, though, gave her a clue as to why the man had chosen their home to burglarize.

Wendell had made good use of his photos, but readers had to open to page three to see them. The photo spread included several of Jimmy Kerrigan, lying on the ground, on a stretcher, and being loaded into an ambulance. The ones of Watts were less graphic, perhaps out of respect for the dead, or for the readers. They included one of the ambulance, a photo of Officer Davis giving an interview, and one of Watts' home in Springfield.

While it seemed to Joy that the articles were complete and well-written, they yielded little new information. Joy sighed. What more could she expect?

Looking through the rest of the news, Joy saw that the high school holiday pageant would be performed Friday night, the choral society concert was set for Saturday, and the children's Christmas parade would be held downtown on Sunday afternoon at two. The last of these events usually brought out most of the town, and was followed by vigorous holiday shopping at the local merchants. For most of a week the dark cloud of the two accidents had hung over her community. Perhaps now their holiday celebrations could proceed unfettered.

***

The weather on Sunday was perfect for the children's parade. While Holly declared herself to be too old to participate in such things, Nick and Joy convinced her to come and watch, with the promise of an ice cream soda at the drug store afterward.

As usual, most of the town was in attendance. Wendell was there with his camera taking photos of the crowd, and awaiting the first group of marchers to come around from the parking lot behind the town hall and begin the route around the green.

Joy looked at the crowd, and noticed most of her guests from the open house were there. The Selectmen huddled together, and several of her coworkers stood with cameras at the ready to take pictures of their children. Even Jimmy Kerrigan's sister was there, surrounded by other women, all wearing red hats. Joy searched the sea of faces. Where was Dr. Barnes? She could not silence her lingering suspicions about the man. Then she looked again at Margaret Kerrigan.

"I've got it!" Joy said, grabbing Nick's arm. "I know what happened."

"Huh?" he said, looking toward the town hall.

"Where's Dan Davis? I need him."

She found Officer Davis working crowd control. She ducked under the yellow tape marking the parade route, stepped over the snow bank, and ran out into the street.

"I'm sorry, Joy, but you'll have to stay behind the tape. The parade will be starting any minute," Officer Davis told her.

The clock in the town hall tower struck two, and Joy could hear the drums of the high school band starting their beat.

"I know, Dan," Joy insisted, "but you need to come with me. I figured it out. I know what happened last weekend, *and* what is probably happening *right now*. We have to get over to 509 West Elm Street. Now!"

She turned and looked up the street. The parade

was just coming around the corner of the town hall. Wendell had his tripod set up, ready to take pictures.

"Wendell," she called. "Bring your camera and come with us!"

Wendell turned and looked at her as if she were crazy.

"Believe me, Wendell. This is one exclusive you will *not* want to miss."

Officer Davis led her to his police car, and with Wendell in the back seat, they sped down Elm Street. Along the way, Joy explained their errand.

"I would never have figured it out without your headline on Thursday, Wendell. The answer is in the two Elm streets."

"What was the question?" Officer Davis asked.

"The question is why Watts picked our house to burglarize, and the answer is he thought it was the Kerrigan's. They live at 509 West Elm, and we live at 509 East Elm. He was an out-of-towner, so he didn't realize there was more than one 509 Elm Street."

"Why would he want to go to the Kerrigan's?" Wendell asked as they pulled up to the address.

"Let's ask him," Joy said, pointing to a Santa standing on the Kerrigan's roof trying to open the skylight.

Davis got out of the car, and, using the door as a shield, drew his gun. "Put your hands in the air and freeze," he shouted, pointing his gun at Santa.

Wendell started snapping pictures out the window. "Joy, I can't get out of here. Open the door for me. I'm missing the shot."

"Stay inside," Davis barked.

Joy opened her door and released Wendell from the back seat.

"Don't shoot," Santa yelled. "I'm unarmed. I don't mean anyone any harm."

"Dr. Barnes?" Wendell said, snapping more pictures. "Is that you?"

Davis called for back-up, and approached the house. "How did you get up there?"

"I have a ladder in the back," Barnes said.

"Okay, then let's walk toward the back, and you come down the ladder, nice and slow."

Officer Davis read him his rights. By the time the back-up arrived, followed by some of the parade crowd, Barnes was in handcuffs, sitting in the back seat of the cruiser. He was spilling his guts, while Wendell took down every word.

"When I got to Kerrigan's house the night of the accident, the old man thought he was a goner. He told me that while he ran his garage, he saved every old coin that came through his till. He said he had a collection worth over a hundred-thousand dollars under a loose floorboard upstairs, and no one knew about it—not even his sister. He wanted me to make sure his sister got them. From the look of him, I thought he probably wouldn't make it, so I called my old buddy, Harry Watts. We'd, uh, done some work together in the past."

Joy gave Wendell a smug look.

"Anyway, Watts was a screw-up. He went to the wrong house, and he died for his trouble. There isn't even a skylight at that other house."

Joy nodded. "Never has been."

"So you came back today to get the coins?" Wendell asked.

"I tried to get them out of my mind. But I figured that after the coma, Kerrigan wouldn't remember telling me about them. Heck, he might not remember that he had them. So, I figured it was worth a try."

"And you picked today, because everyone would be at the parade," Joy said.

"Yeah. I hate parades, but it seemed like such a big deal in this town that I figured none of the neighbors would be home to see me here. And I dressed as

Santa because Watts said if he did that and moved around like a robot, anyone who saw him would think he was just a mechanical Christmas decoration. It sounded like a good idea to me."

Joy rolled her eyes. "We may be small town, but we're not idiots."

"You didn't have to go to all that trouble," Davis said. "Like too many people in this town, the Kerrigans never lock their doors. You could have just gone inside."

***

The following Thursday, the *Town Monitor* sold every copy. "Caught Red-Suited," read another of Wendell's classic headlines. But the story of Dr. Barnes' criminal ways did not end in their small town. The Springfield police came up to talk to him while he sat in county jail. It looked like Dr. Barnes would not be celebrating Christmas without bars on his windows for a very long time.

"Now, what was that you were saying about me having an over-active imagination?" Joy said, handing the paper to Nick.

"I guess it turned out to be a good thing that you do," Nick said with a wink.

"Uh, you guys," Holly said. "You know you still owe me an ice cream soda."

Christmas Memories

Emily P. W. Murphy

"*M*iss. Miss!" The elderly woman calls from across the room. I hang the final ornament on her artificial Christmas tree and survey my work before moving in her direction.

"Miss!" She calls again as I walk toward her wheelchair. She points her finger, knobby with arthritis, in my direction, as if to prevent me from ignoring her.

"Is there something you need?" I ask when I know I'm close enough for her to hear without my having to shout.

She pans her finger away to point at a screen mounted on the wall nearby. "My TV is broken."

I look to where she is pointing, at a digital picture frame, not a television. But I do not argue.

"Would you like me to fix it?" I ask her before moving to turn it on.

The woman nods with a vigor that seems out of place in a person her age. The skin that droops beneath her chin swings with the movement, but her permed white curls stay locked in place.

"My program is about to start," she insists.

I reach behind the frame and my fingers find the power switch. I press and the frame lights up with a picture of a woman in her mid-sixties, her hair more than a little gray. Beneath the picture, in bold, sans-serif print, the caption reads: YOUR DAUGHTER. The woman in the picture smiles at us for fifteen seconds before she is replaced by a picture of a similar-looking man. This caption reads: YOUR SON.

I sit in a nearby chair to watch two granddaughters appear on the screen.

The woman clamps her toothless gums together and her lips mush out in front of her. "I have a daughter, you know," she says. The picture changes to a third granddaughter.

"Is that so?"

"Her name is Josie," the woman says nodding her head. "She's ten. She's at school right now, but she'll be home soon."

I don't point out to the woman that in order for her to have a ten-year-old she would have had to have given birth at the age of eighty-three. I don't point out that it's Sunday, or that it's Christmas Eve, or that it's night and we can see the stars and the reflection of the moon on the fresh snow through the window in the room. I just smile and nod.

Now the picture labeled: YOUR GRANDSON dissolves to reveal a picture of a baby. The caption reads: YOUR GREAT-GRANDSON.

The woman scrunches up her face. "What an ugly baby," she says. "Why'd they cast such an ugly baby?"

I shrug. I have no answer to her question.

The picture of the baby disappears and is replaced by a group shot of the entire family.

"Mom," the caption reads, "we will love you even when you can't remember who we are. And we know you'll still love us, too."

The woman reads the words. She reaches up and scratches her cheek and I notice how thin the skin is on the back of her hand, her veins purple and dark. I stand, and look back at the screen. The show has started again. My face, once again, looks out at us, smiling.

"Merry Christmas, Mom," I say bending to kiss my mother on the head. She doesn't notice. Her world has no place for strangers like me.

Christmas Folly

Sally Wyman Paradysz

*M*y friends and I have a tradition. Or perhaps you'd call it a ritual. Every month without fail, on the twenty-third day, we meet to talk. Really talk. Our ritual is not one of idle conversation; it is not a time to discuss the exploits of celebrities, or to gossip. Instead, on this scheduled day, my five best friends and I meet to discuss ourselves. We look deep into our hearts, and into our souls. Together we look at our challenges, helping each other to work them out, and gain strength during the process. We meet at each others' homes. Each of us hosts twice in the course of the year.

I awake on December twenty-third to a constant, yet familiar, noise. Listening, eyes closed, I try to bring back the memory.

Awareness begins to seep in: this is not my bed. Lazily opening my eyes and looking around my studio, I notice the tell-tale signs, and laugh at my folly. Coffee cups, stale crackers, cheese, and a red-stained wine glass complete my picture. Working late into the night, I fell asleep on the day-bed under the windows. But it is the sound that pulls me up. Wrapping the blanket around my shoulders, I peer out at the vicious, howling, wind-slapping snowstorm, raging against my windowpanes.

"Oh my," I say to no one, climbing off the bed. The storm is both unexpected and breathtaking. Cold and stiff, I walk toward the bathroom at the rear of the room.

"No heat," I mumble, flipping the light switch up and down several times. "Electric is off, damn it—no coffee, no heat, and no food."

But the light is perfect right now. My need to create is greater than any other physical need, so I go back to my palette and easel.

Looking up four hours later, I find it is mid-afternoon, and I'm shivering. I need to get out of the studio and into the house. I have to make a fire in my woodstove to bring some warmth to my body. Food and coffee would be good. I pull on my down coat and boots, ready to brave the weather.

I can hardly see the shape of the house with the snow blowing in my face and eyes, but I manage to grasp the rope and pull myself along. Being from New England, I understand winter, and I've learned tricks to make things easier. One is tying a rope from the tree outside my studio to the screened porch on my small cottage home, wrapping it around trees as I go, keeping it taut and off the ground.

Bent at the waist, and holding the rope line, I make my way against the gale winds. The woods stand strong, but I can hear small branches falling into the snow with soft thuds.

Passing by the shed, I duck in and grab one of the buckets, filling it to the brim with seed and corn. I refill the bird feeders and deer feeding stations closest to the house. Making it onto the screened porch, I place the empty container safely beside the wood holder.

My friends are coming this evening, and I must get the house ready, stoking up the woodstove, and placing candles around the room. It is my turn to host this month. I look forward to these nights, and want to make my home especially cozy, to welcome the difficult and intimate conversations we sometimes share. Each of us has her own story to tell.

Good thing the meeting is here tonight. I am the only one with a woodstove, and a gas range, so not only can I offer heat, I can also make a huge pot of hot stew for these precious friends of mine.

Each winter, I fill several five-gallon containers with water for drinking, and put them in the basement in case the electricity goes out. Knowing I have extra water feels good on days like today; I can cook or bake anything. And the screened porch doubles as an extra refrigerator.

Life in a small New England town gives me everything my heart needs. The winters are beautiful even in their harshness, and my wood stove gathers my friends on cold and snowy days.

Stomping my feet, I barge into my study from the porch. *Cold*, I think. I can see my breath. Shivering again, I take off my coat and pull on the heavy wool sweater hanging by my reading chair. It takes a moment for my body to warm it up. Rubbing my hands together, I head toward the woodstove in the living room. My wood holder is full, and small pieces of kindling fill the box nearby. Only a moment or two passes before a blazing fire warms the silent room.

The only thing I'll miss tonight will be a hot shower, I muse. Instead, I get to work bringing up one of the water containers, pouring some into a huge pot on the stove. When it's warm, I can use it to bathe, and wash my hair, and be refreshed when the girls arrive.

Once I am clean, I set about making dinner. I pull out my mother's cast iron skillet to make corn bread. Then I combine a multitude of veggies in a pot to make my stew. Onions, garlic, potatoes, broccoli, greens,

carrots, corn, and all of them roasted yesterday; perfect. Add stock and simmer. All made within the hour.

As daylight fades into early evening, cozy is the word of the night, and I can't wait for my friends to arrive. I love hosting our December meetings; it's my own tradition to volunteer for this month, one of the longest nights of the year. My Christmas tree sits in a corner, between the window and the sliding door to the deck. The glow of the woodstove and candles makes it appear magical.

Before everyone arrives, I bring six heavy soup bowls over to the woodstove and warm them. Sitting down for a moment in front of the tree, I picture the evening ahead; legs flopping over armrests, cushions scattered around the room, and wine glasses everywhere. "Lordy, I love these friends," I whisper. "They inspire me so much."

I admire Gail's tenacity, Jackie's boldness, Alex's fortitude, Terri's sense of humor, and Sandy's naiveté.

I think back to Gail, and how hard she fought turning the farm into a successful boarding stable after her husband's unexpected death. My hands held hers as she slipped in and out of courage over the years, but now she has arrived as a strong and prosperous woman.

I think back to one summer evening, when we gathered around Jackie's backyard fire pit.

"Hey you guys, time to take the bras off. This party doesn't end until the last woman gets to say her piece," Jackie said, her expression grave.

I remember laughing. "Yep, that's pretty much the way we work around here." We sat holding each other's hands, crying or laughing, depending on the next friend's story.

"Never underestimate the power of the women around this fire," Jackie said later when the fire burned low, and the night enveloped us. "We have all learned to make time for everything important. We need to continue to count on each other for support."

Yes, that was an important evening. I'm hopeful this night will bring more of that intimate conversation, so essential to each of us.

I remember another touching meeting in August. Sandy came to the gathering having just watched her little girl drive away to college.

"The hard part is the damned recognition of how quickly life passes," she whispered to us, crying tears of tenderness as she recounted the experience. When the tears subsided, she went on, "There just doesn't seem to be enough time for everything. What we are most passionate about often gets left out of life. I want to be a writer, and I don't know how to fit that into my already hectic schedule."

I remember many conversations over the years. They are each treasures, and I hold onto them for comfort.

Now the house is filled with the aroma of stew, gently simmering in the kitchen. Thinking back again to Sandy, I realize she has now completed her first book, and is on to the next. Tonight we must help her gather the courage to let the manuscript go, and celebrate the completion of it; not the writing of it. It is the completion of something she earned through effort and passion that is important. All of us will urge her forward, gently and with love.

The electricity gives a burp of life, and then dies again. Secretly I wish it will stay off for a while longer. We don't need it tonight. We will be okay with each other, food, and warmth. Oh, and the wine. Don't forget the wine!

I wait for my friends, sitting on the rug in front of the tree and stove. "Thank you God for helping me to become my greatest self," I whisper into the tree. "Each moment is a new moment, and I can't wait for the challenge of all of them." I am sure the Christmas tree hears my secrets, as it stands strong and beautiful and lovely.

I hear Terri's 4 Runner rumble up my driveway, and know my friends are all here. She always picks everyone up during the winter months. Nothing can stop her. "No fear in that woman," I say, as I rise from the floor.

My friends are giggling and laughing softly as I walk out of my home to greet them in the snow. *We are gifted with each other*, I think, as I look at each of them running toward me with arms outstretched for a hug.

Terri's the first one into my arms. She holds up wine bottles—she always brings the wine—and then makes straight for the opener. It is always her job to pour and distribute the goblets. I wonder what tonight's toasts will uncover, as we each lift a glass. At Christmastime, things are usually more subdued. But not always. With the storm blowing outside, and the warmth of the blazing fire, you never know what will come of the evening.

Alex is next into the house, followed by Sandy, Gail, and Jackie.

This group of women takes my breath away with all their determination and effort. They are loving, strong, and are my chosen women family. Each of them stands in her own truth, and lives each day as if the devil himself is after her.

Once inside, we pour the wine, and offer the toasts. Each of us grabs a seat or throws a pillow on the floor to sit or lie on. Whatever works, there are no rules. The aroma of the stew is making everyone crazy hungry, so I bring the pot over to the woodstove and place it on the trivet resting there. Terri, my CPA, walks behind me with a large dipping spoon, corn bread, and cloth napkins. We break bread together.

***

After dinner, everyone groans, filled to the brim, having overindulged.

"What's for dessert?" Gail asks, laughing.

"Wine!" Terri grins.

Within the intimacy of friends, the evening goes its way. We open another wine bottle, and more laughter follows. No one has too much to drink, because each prefers to be present, feeling the love given and shared. Feelings of coziness and strength come within the familiarity, and time doesn't fly by, it glides.

I marvel at the way each of my friends seems to have found her own gifts. They are amazing. Life holds excitement for all of us, but we gather our strength from this group as a whole. Together, we honor our passions; they are what life is all about, at any age.

The wind howls and snow continues to build its layers, as my friends leave together into the starless stormy night. All of our secrets and tears will stay within our hearts.

"I promise to call after I drop everyone off," Terri yells running out the door. "I want you to know how the roads are in case you need to go out." She knows my whims better than I, but then she has been included in many of them in the past.

As I slip into bed with my cell phone, I wait for Terri's call. The room is darker than usual because of the snow-covered skylight, but there is some reflected light coming in off the snow through the windows by my bed. Lying here all warm and cozy, I fall into a deep sleep.

I awake hours later to the buzz of my phone's

voicemail, and realize I never heard Terri's call come in. Listening to the message, I start to laugh.

"Hi, Sal. Let's meet at seven o'clock so we can watch the sunrise together. The storm has passed," Terri's sleepy voice says. I look at my clock; it is only six thirty. I can just make it to our favorite spot.

Grabbing my sweats, coat, and boots, I'm out the door and into the cold, clear, early-morning darkness. Taking gloves from my pocket, I yank open my old truck door and start the engine. While it warms, I brush off the eight inches of fluffy new snow. When the truck is ready, I ease my way down the driveway and out to the street beyond my woods. A town plow has already come through, so I drive the back roads to the lake.

"This is so much fun," I say, and laugh out loud.

We arrive at the same time. As Terri climbs into my warm truck she opens a steamy thermos of black coffee. "Perfect," I say. I ask if everyone got home safely last night.

"Why, of course. I was driving." Terri says, turning to me with a wink and a smirk.

Everything is so still and pristine. After another cup of coffee we open the doors, climb out into the snow, and walk to the edge of the lake. It is ice-covered at the edge, but open in the middle.

As we stand there together, Terri takes hold of my hand and says, "Look, the sun is just peeking out above the water. It looks so gorgeous. Merry Christmas Eve, Sal."

"Merry Christmas Eve to you, Terri, my friend." Side by side, we watch the sun rise until it clears the trees. Then we scamper back into the truck to get warm. After watching nature awaken for another hour we leave the lake, each to our own tasks for the day.

As long as I'm out, I stop by the feed store. Everyone is wishing each other a Merry Christmas, and sharing hugs and smiles. When it is my turn at the counter I order a hundred pounds of cracked corn, and fifty pounds of premium bird seed, and wait inside while the boys throw the fifty pound bags into the back of my pickup. When they are finished, I drive back home, slipping and sliding up my driveway to the shed. Putting it all away, I notice there are two twenty-five pound bags of puppy food among the bird seed and corn. "Whoops," I say. "The boys made a mistake." I leave it in the shed to return after Christmas. I'm too tired to drive back now. All I want is a hot shower if the electricity is back on.

Walking into my little home, I hear the humming of the refrigerator.

"Yippee," I yell, dancing up the stairs to my bathroom, and turning on the tap.

The water is so hot it steams up the glass enclosure, and the skylights above. I relax and lean back for a good soak. My eyes are closed when I hear a noise from outside the glass. Rubbing the steamy walls with my hands, I am more than surprised when a puppy stares back at me! *A Sheltie puppy, my favorite.*

"Well, who are you?" I ask with delight. Shutting off the shower and opening the door I grab for a towel, but not fast enough. The puppy gets into the shower, and soon her feet are soaking wet. Then she makes a beeline for my bed. "Oh no," I yell, "not the bed!" But up she goes, running around in circles until the spot is right, then she curls up in the middle looking straight into my eyes.

Just then, I hear giggles and laughs that are very familiar. The girls are at it again, bouncing into my room and onto my bed. I stand there, mouth open, wrapped in a towel.

"Merry Christmas, Sal," they all say in unison.

Speechless, I turn and walk back into the bathroom to get dressed, shaking my head.

It is quiet when I go back into my bedroom; my five friends are all sitting on my bed, petting the puppy, and looking at me with questioning eyes. I stand there, hands on hips, saying nothing. The next moment I hop onto my bed, and with peals of laughter we all hug.

"Merry Christmas, ladies." I giggle. I take a breath and steady my voice. "So, what is this puppy doing here?"

"She is our gift to you this year," Jackie says, speaking for the group. "You've done so much for each of us that we want to give back."

Terri grinned, "We remembered when you mentioned this past summer that you wanted a Sheltie puppy, and we thought this was the perfect time to buy one for you. I know you might have wanted to pick one out yourself, but all of us got together yesterday and fell in love with this little girl. We were going to bring her over last night for the meeting, but she was so cute we knew we'd never spend time talking."

"You're right," I say. "Who could talk seriously with something this cute licking your face?"

"Do you love her?" they ask.

"Come here little girl, and let me look you over." I pick her up, and hold her in my arms; soon she is looking at me and snuggling into my chest for a good sleep. As I hug her quietly I look at my friends, one by one.

"Her name will be Frosty," I say, smiling through my tears, "and I love her already. Thank you for this precious gift. I wondered what the puppy food was doing in my truck with the other feed. Now I know. I should have known you guys would be involved in something like this."

I carry Frosty downstairs and place her on a blanket under the tree. She opens her eyes for a second, yawns, and closes them again.

Quietly and respectfully each person leaves, having one last peek at the new puppy. After filling the woodstove and yanking the winter quilt from my reading chair, I snuggle under the tree with my new Christmas gift.

"You and I are going to share a lifetime together, because of our treasured friends," I say, pulling her gently into my arms. "We have each other to rely on now, and we are very blessed.

"Merry Christmas, sweet love," I whisper into her soft, warm fur.

Pickle's Christmas Wonder

Will Wright

*T*he North Pole has the finest bear school in the world. Pickle, Thistle, Taffy, and Bowser were very excited to learn all about being bears. They were not going to be just regular bears, either. They were going to be Christmas bears!

Buddy Bear was the teacher of bear school. He had been a Christmas bear when he was new. Santa made Buddy the teacher because his friend, Lynn, read him every story there was about Santa and the North Pole.

You see, bears, no matter how smart they get, still need their people to read to them.

Pickle, Thistle, Taffy, and Bowser learned how to bring sweet dreams, and to keep the bed bugs from biting. They learned how to turn a smile into a giggle, and a giggle into a laugh. They learned how to soak up tears and turn them into love.

And they learned about the Christmas Wonder.

"Every year," said Buddy, "each boy or girl who believes in Santa gets one Christmas Wonder."

"Is it a warm feeling?" asked Pickle.

"Is it a funny tickle?" asked Thistle.

"Is it a happy sigh?" asked Taffy.

"Is it something to eat?" asked Bowser.

"It can be anything," said Buddy, "though I never heard of one that was something to eat. As Christmas bears, it is our job to wish for our boy or girl to get the best Christmas Wonder possible."

"How do we do that?" asked Pickle.

"We do it," said Buddy, "by wishing for what's best for our boy or girl, no matter what–even if it's not good for us."

"Even if it's not good for us?" said Pickle, Thistle, Taffy, and Bowser.

"Christmas bears are unselfish," said Buddy, "because they love so much."

It was the hardest thing that Pickle learned at bear school. How do you want something for someone else even if it's not good for you? He almost didn't take his *pie ursa bearra* diploma at graduation.

"Don't worry," said Buddy Bear. "The secret is love."

Holly, the elf, led the new graduates to Santa's great hall where there were many toys, puzzles, candies and treats waiting for Santa to decide where each gift would go.

"Today we learn the name of the boy or girl we will go to on Christmas day!" said Thistle.

Thistle went to a girl named Chrissy. Taffy went to a girl named Danielle. Bowser went to a boy named Spike. Pickle was happy for his friends, but was sad to see them go.

"Now," said Santa, "this next list is for a boy named Willie. Willie is three years old, and he believes in me."

"That means he gets a Christmas Wonder," said Pickle to the peppermint candy cane next to him.

"Shush!" said the candy cane. "I want to hear this!"

"On Christmas," said Santa, "Willie will get Pepper the candy cane, Loopy the lollypop, Pickle the bear, and Reginald the fire truck."

"My boy's name is Willie!" said Pickle.

"He's my boy, too," said the candy cane who had shushed him before. "But Willie's getting a fire truck. That just means I'll end up in a candy dish, and you'll collect dust under the bed."

Pickle didn't think that Pepper was very friendly.

"Oh don't mind him," said a lollypop behind him. "He's just an old stick in the mint." The lollypop hopped over Pickle's head, and balanced on his stick.

"I'm Loopy," he said.

"I'm Pickle," said Pickle. "It is very nice to meet you."

"I wouldn't know," said Loopy. "I've never met me before."

Pickle decided that Loopy was a little confusing, but he was a very friendly lollypop.

"Clang, clang, clang."

There was a big, red, toy fire truck behind Pickle. It was one of the biggest toys in Santa's hall–even bigger than most of the tricycles.

"My name is Reginald," said the fire truck. "If your name's Pickle, hop up on my running board and hang on!"

Pickle did just that, and Reginald sped off so fast that Pickle's cloth ears folded back in the wind.

"You've got a good grip," said Reginald. "That's a good thing, 'cause I think we'll be doing this a lot when we get to Willie's house. Clang, clang, clang!"

"Hey! Where's the fire?" Pepper grumbled as they circled around him.

"That's not much of a Yule spirit, Pepper," said Loopy. "Are you sure you're a candy cane and not a misshaped sour ball?"

Pickle very much liked riding on Reginald. He was a very fine fire truck, so big and fast and pretty.

"Willie is very fortunate to get such a wonderful toy," said Pickle.

"Yeah," said Loopy hopping up and down on his stick. "Willie will be crazy about him. He'll be Willie's Christmas Wonder."

"Yeah," said Pepper. "Willie will wonder why Santa even bothered bringing us."

"Douse that kind of talk!" said Reginald. "Christmas is supposed to be fun. Willie will have fun with all of us!"

"But Loopy is right," said Pickle. "You're sure to be Willie's Christmas Wonder."

"I know you can sure lick me," said Loopy.

"I don't care what Willie's Christmas Wonder is," said Reginald. "I just hope that he likes to have fun—and go really fast! Clang, clang, clang!"

Holly, the elf, walked up with a big sack.

"It's time to go in Santa's sack," said Holly

"The sack's too small," said Pepper. "Reginald won't even fit in there all by himself."

"It's a magic sack," said Holly, and she picked up Reginald and threw him inside. Reginald didn't stick out at all, but Pickle could hear, "clang, clang, clang!" coming from inside.

Pickle thought that Santa's sack would be dark and crowded, but it wasn't like that at all. There were more toys than he could count inside and everyone was singing "Deck the Halls" and "Jingle Bells." Pickle found Thistle, Taffy, and Bowser, and the bears sang in four-part harmony like they learned at bear school.

When they got to Willie's house, Santa pulled Pickle, Pepper, Loopy, and Reginald out of his sack. He hung Pepper on the Christmas tree. He looked very pretty with a Christmas light behind him. Then Santa put a big bow around Reginald together with a sign that said, "To Willie from Santa," and put him in the middle of the room. Then he put Loopy and Pickle, side-by-side, at the top of Willie's stocking.

"That looks just about right," said Santa.

Pickle looked at the room. Reginald was so big and shiny. Willie would never even notice Loopy and him at the top of the stocking.

Santa clucked Pickle under the chin, and it made the bear laugh.

"That's better," said Santa. "Now remember, Pickle, you have a job to do."

"I'm supposed to wish for Willie to have the best Christmas Wonder possible."

"That's right," said Santa.

"But, Santa," said Pickle, "Reginald will be Willie's Christmas Wonder, and Reginald said he doesn't even care. He just wants to have fun and go fast."

"That's Reginald's job," said Santa. "But Christmas bears have a different job, and you're a Christmas bear. Remember what Buddy taught you, and you'll do fine."

So instead of feeling sorry for himself, Pickle started wishing. He didn't worry about anything else— even if he ended up under the bed collecting dust. All that mattered was that Willie have a great Christmas Wonder. It didn't matter if that Wonder was a funny tickle, a happy sigh, a warm feeling, or something to eat. It didn't matter if the Wonder was a big, shiny, fast fire truck that went clang, clang, clang. What mattered was that Willie's Christmas Wonder was a wonderful Wonder.

So all night long, Pickle wished and wished and wished some more, until sunlight came through the window and he heard little feet on the stairs.

"Oh boy!" said Reginald. "We're going to have fun!"

"Fun?" said Pepper. "Like having a Christmas tree light melt my stripes all night?"

"Oh look," said Loopy. "He just came around the corner. He's so cute! I'm a sucker for him already."

Pickle looked across the room at three-year-old Willie with his bright eyes and curly hair, and something happened inside. Pickle's little bear heart started beating and wouldn't stop.

And each little beat said, "I love you."

Willie ran across the room, jumped over the big, new fire truck, and pulled Pickle out of the stocking.

"You smiled at me," said Willie. "Mommy, the teddy bear smiled at me."

"That's because it's Christmas," said Willie's mother. "Wonders happen at Christmas—especially with Christmas bears."

That night, Willie's mother looked in on her little boy. He was hugging Pickle the bear tight. A silly lollypop looked down at the two from the bedpost. A shiny new fire truck was resting at the foot of the bed. It needed the rest. The truck had gone fast and had fun all day long.

Willie's mother went back down stairs, gathered up the candy canes, and put them in a candy dish—even one whose stripes looked like they were melted—and then she sat down and put her head on the chest of her oldest friend. She listened for his heart.

Each little beat said, "I love you."

"Did you have a good time with Santa at the North Pole?" she asked.

"I did," said Buddy, "but it's good to be home."

"It's good to have you home," said Willie's mother whose name was Lynn. "And thank you for my little boy's Christmas Wonder."

Walter and Stella

Ralph Hieb

*W*alter wondered where the Christmas spirit had gone.

Since he first woke up. Walter couldn't get anyone to acknowledge him. They only stared without mumbling a word. He could see from their red-rimmed eyes that they had been crying, but he didn't know why. "Please," he begged. "Just tell me what's wrong. Why isn't anyone speaking, and why all the crying?"

Walking over to the television he bent down to talk to Tommy, his great-grandson. Tommy was only two, but he always had time to talk to Pop-Pop.

"Hey, Tommy, what are you watching?" When the cartoon characters started to sing a song, Tommy joined in. "Come on, Tommy. Can you give Pop-Pop a hug?" Walter held out his arms to the boy. The hope and joy he always felt radiated through the wrinkled face that smiled down at the child. Tommy looked in his direction and smiled, then turned back to the colorful singing animals.

"Well at least you acknowledged me," Walter said. Disappointed, he turned and observed the table set for the holiday feast. The red and green tablecloth with its scene of a sleigh pulled through the snow by a single horse had always seemed to be part of the season. Now it just looked old and worn. A spray of evergreens with some holly mixed in was set in the center of the cloth, the bright colors doing nothing for the inhabitants of the room.

Walter always enjoyed Christmas, but something didn't seem right this year. The happiness that he had shared with the family was missing. The glumness of the gathering was driving him to despair.

"I don't' understand it." Walter shrugged his shoulders. "Just the other day everyone was talking to me and we were all having a great time. Then suddenly no one knows I exist." Depressed, he turned toward the living room. Suddenly seeing a lone figure sitting on the couch staring blankly at the show Tommy was watching, Walter gasped.

"Ryan!" he yelled excitedly. "When did you get back? I thought your tour in Iraq wasn't supposed to end until next month. I bet Grandma, Judy, and the kids are happy to see you." Despite the excitement Walter displayed, Ryan didn't stop staring. "Ryan, what's wrong boy? You and me have always been the best of friends." Ryan shivered slightly and looked at the floor, not saying a word. Now Walter didn't know whether to be frustrated or angry. His family was ignoring him; something he never allowed was people to slight someone who talked to them. Starting to shake with rage, he stopped when he heard the gentle voice coming from the hallway.

"Hello, everyone." Her voice was as delicate as the softly-falling snow. Looking at her, Walter's eyes filled with tears.

Stella walked slowly into the room, with their daughter holding her arm to steady her. Taking a step toward them, Walter smiled. Even as old as Stella was, to Walter she still seemed the beautiful young bride that he had married over sixty years ago.

"Stella," Walter called. "Stella." He raised his voice. "Please darling, you should have worn your hearing aid, or has the battery gone dead again?" He started in her direction then stopped, afraid if he got in the way she might fall. "Just take your time and sit," he added lovingly.

Ryan's wife, Judy, helped her husband's grandmother into the chair at the head of the table. Walter's place at the other end was empty. "Well if nobody's going to talk to me, I might as well sit and stare like the rest of you."

Walking to the head of the table Walter stopped. "Stella," he said gently. "Please, honey, what's wrong with everyone?"

Looking at his wife, Walter saw the silver lines of tears running down her face. "Please, honey. Just tell me what's wrong. I promise I'll do whatever it takes to fix it.

"I see Ryan is home for the holidays. He won't talk to me either. Only Tommy looks at me, and then he only smiles."

The light in the room grew brighter; Walter could see a radiance that illuminated the Christmas tree, making it sparkle and glow with more intensity than he had ever seen. Its brilliance seemed to beckon for him to come closer.

"Stella have you ever seen a tree as bright and beautiful as this one?"

Stella just continued to cry as she faced the table, her shoulders shaking slightly, the soft sobs muffled by the handkerchief she held to her face.

Walter moved around to kneel in front of her.

"Stella," he whispered. "Please tell me what's wrong." As he reached out to hold her, Walter realized that he was kneeling *in* the table. Looking slowly from one side to the other, he gasped. "Oh, my. That pain in my chest." He hesitated. "Could it have been?" Looking up at Stella, he nodded. "It had to have been a heart attack. I'm so sorry, Stella. I never meant to leave you alone. Can you forgive me?"

Walter's shoulders hunched as he looked at the floor. "Why did it take so long for me to know? I thought it was only yesterday, but it must have been a week ago." Looking up at the ceiling with tears running down his face he whispered, "Why? Why did it take so long for me to come back and see them? I want them to be happy, to celebrate my life, not to mourn."

"I just need to lie down." Stella's voice was frail, but Judy heard and helped the elderly woman to her bedroom.

Not knowing what to do, Walter stood looking at his family. Now he understood why Ryan was home from the war. "I guess that old wives' tale about little children being able to see the dead is true. Isn't it, Tommy?"

The youngster looked in his direction. "Op-Op." He smiled, and then looked back at his cartoons.

Walking over to the Christmas tree, Walter studied its ornaments. The tree glowed again. "I think I know what you're trying to tell me. But I'm not going anywhere without my Stella." The light dimmed again.

Taking a deep breath, Walter walked to the kitchen window and gazed longingly at the snow-covered swing set. Hedges that lined the yard were now lifeless sticks reaching for the sky. Off on the side sat the shed. When spring came, layers of flowers of every color would surround it. As the weather got warmer, Stella would carefully move the soil from on top of her prize roses so that they would be able to reestablish themselves. She so loved those roses and her garden. Walter wondered how much longer she would have the strength to toil in the yard as she had done for so many years.

The holly bushes were still giving off a Christmas look; their bright, green leaves were adorned with radiant, red berries. A fluffy coating of snow made the rest of the yard look at peace.

Looking back at the Christmas tree, standing proudly in front of the large picture window, Walter imagined what wonderful presents awaited Tommy. The boxes with their images of Santa and his reindeer signified the gifts for the youngster; the gifts with bright metallic wrapping were for the adults.

"Grams is sleeping so peacefully," Judy told everyone at the table. "I think we should let her rest. When she wakes up, I'll fix her a plate."

"I guess that's best. She hasn't slept well for a while," Ryan agreed.

Walter stood there as the family had a quiet dinner. He never moved as Judy and the other women cleared the table and set out dessert. As the shadows of night fell, he watched a few birds pick at the scraps of bread that Tommy had tossed out for them. The only time Walter smiled was when Tommy giggled at the birds that came to claim his offerings.

After the family went to bed, the house

was completely dark. The silence became overpowering, making Walter want to scream. Still, he stood looking out into the small yard that had given him and Stella years of enjoyment. He remembered watching their children grow up there; then the grandchildren coming to visit; and now the thrill of seeing Tommy, their great-grandson, laugh as he ran around the yard while slow-moving adults never seemed able to catch him.

Behind Walter, the Christmas tree, once again, started to glimmer. Its beacon grew more intense than it had at any time during the day, brightly lighting the room.

"I already told you," Walter said, "I'm not going anywhere."

"Why not?" came a soft voice from behind him.

Turning, Walter saw Stella silhouetted in front of the tree.

As he stepped closer, her features became clear. It wasn't the Stella that Walter had seen needing help to make it to the bedroom. In front of him stood the young, strong Stella that he had married all those years ago.

"Stella, honey, you can see me?"

"Yes dear. I can see you. And I can hear you. I wasn't going to stay here alone, so I've come to you."

"By all that is merciful, you're young and healthy again." Walter took her outstretched hands into his. Tears ran down Walter's face. "I don't deserve the love of someone as beautiful as you. You're so young."

"Walter, look at your hands. They're as strong as they ever were."

Looking at his hands, Walter could see that the age spots were gone. Wrinkles and arthritis were no longer visible. Fingers that had been bent into useless angles were straight and firm. He opened and closed his hands flexing the now functional append-ages. "How can this be?"

"I don't know, but this is the first time in years that I can lift my arms without them hurting." Stella posed with her arms over her head, and then lowered them. Waving her hands up and down, she reminded Walter of a bird, landing gracefully.

As they stood looking into each other's eyes, the room became even brighter. "Come, you two. Stop lollygagging about." The voice came from the center of the light. Walter could see his mother as he remembered her when he was a child. Family members, long dead, stood around her. Mixed in with them were Stella's ancestors.

Walter and Stella stood transfixed before them. Smiling, Walter's mother explained, "Everyone here appears as they wish to be seen. Their health returns, and we can celebrate every holiday together, forever."

Taking both of Stella's hands into his own, Walter said, "This is the best Christmas present ever. Together and healthy."

Turning, they both looked into the light. Walter rubbed his hands on his jacket, then, looking at Stella, he held out his hand. Smiling, they walked, hand in hand, into the light.

Auld Lang Syne

Jo Ann Schaffer

The hands resting on her husband's chart were impeccably groomed. She couldn't take her eyes off them. The spell was broken only when the anesthesiologist launched into a discussion of "the quality of pain." Had she heard him right? Marty seemed to be listening intently, but she caught the flicker of his eyes in her direction.

It wasn't until they'd gotten into the cab that Marty let loose.

"Quality of pain! Quality bullshit is more like it. What kind of sadist equates pain with quality?"

The diatribe went on for several minutes. Janet said little; there was room for only one person on that soapbox. It was better that he vent his frustrations, but the outburst would also siphon off much of her husband's strength. The experimental medication he was on didn't leave him with much to spare.

As she saw it, her job was to keep him fighting, to tempt him with the sweet flavors of life. The twenty-four year gap in their ages had narrowed considerably since his diagnosis. Now she would take the lead, scraping together the shards of anger and fear, molding them into something beautiful, into a future.

The day after Thanksgiving, she'd struggled through the door with the biggest Christmas tree she could carry. Marty sat in his chair, watching as she danced around the tree to bouncy Christmas tunes, flinging tinsel at the top branches.

"I may not be the most observant Jew, babe," he said, his eyes twinkling, "but isn't it a bit early for the Hanukah bush?"

"Fa-la-la-la-laaaah, you old humbug," she sang as she arranged strands of tinsel over his newly bald head.

She spent trips to the library foraging for anything that might nourish their flagging hopes. Returning home, she would drop her bulging backpack next to the bed. They read long into the night, arguing the merit or folly of unproven therapies, acupuncture, homeopathic cure-alls, or visualization techniques.

"Imagine we're strolling along the soft, white sands of Maui, hon," she'd urge her husband as they struggled to the bathroom during those final weeks.

"A Hawaiian beach I could handle, babe. It's this quicksand that's the problem," he grumbled, squeezing her hand.

He'd endured another torturous nine months, until the drugs mercifully shoved his consciousness aside.

Now it was her turn. Twelve years had not blunted the memory of Marty's illness, and she feared the "quality" her own pain would garner. This time, the prognosis was less dire. Scar tissue from her first back surgery had transformed a mildly annoying numbness into a stabbing pain that thrust and parried with every step. Now a second disk had ruptured.

They'd been arguing for nearly twenty minutes. Janet was adamant, no more surgery. The neurosurgeon rose from his seat, walked around the desk, and sat in the chair beside her.

"Look, Janet," he said with a sigh, "we can continue to find a solution for the pain." His voice sounded as if he were at the far end of tunnel. "It's like this: you're only forty-eight. If we do nothing, within two years you will lose the use of your legs. So what's it going to be: repair the disk or spend the rest of your days in a wheelchair?"

With tears sliding down her cheeks, she slowly nodded. "Tell me what I have to do."

***

"Walk, walk, walk," she repeated, with feigned enthusiasm, standing before the bathroom mirror. It was the mantra she'd received from the physical therapist. She needed to build up her muscles before the surgery, and walking was less torturous than the exercises inflicted upon her at the clinic. But it wasn't much of a rallying cry.

Stepping out of the elevator, she slowly made her way through the lobby, past the enormous artificial spruce with its gaudy trimmings of silver and gold. It had taken a couple of hours to cajole her body into walking mode. Even so, a snail could have easily streaked past her.

Turning back was not an option—not yet. It had taken too long to ease herself into enough layers to ward off the sharp gusts of arctic air schussing down the ice-choked Hudson. Christmas was throwing her a lifeline, and she meant to grab it.

They were always the first in their crowd to get into the swing of the holiday season. Marty loved the spectacle and sentimentality of the Yuletide, even if it wasn't technically his holiday. He always managed to get seats close to the stage for the Christmas show at Radio City. The Rockettes, with their synchronized scissor-kicks, were his idea of a cultural treasure.

"With legs like those, what's not to love about Christmas?" he'd say with a chuckle.

She'd been thinking a lot about that last holiday with Marty. However silly her over-the-top seasonal fervor, it had spurred him to try harder. This year, she needed an extra large dose of treacly holiday spirit. She needed it badly. And she knew just where to find it.

***

As she limped down Broadway, then along the southern edge of Central Park, the stops she planned for her Christmas pilgrimage began to dwindle. The noon organ recital at St. Thomas's was the first to go. The stairs to the nave were impossibly steep, and it would take a mighty tug to open the massive oak door. She fingered the vial of Percocet in her pocket. It was only there for moral support. Next year. The concert would be even sweeter next year.

Turning onto Sixth Avenue, she looked east. Swaying gently over the intersection of Fifth Avenue and Fifty-Seventh Street, suspended between Tiffany's and Bulgari, was the giant crystal snowflake, a stunningly extravagant Christmas bijou from her beloved city.

Propping herself against a parked car, out of the way of the people walking past in double-quick time, she stared at the glowing geometric form and her spirits rose.

"Jay-Jay!" someone yelled.

Her heart sank. Walking towards her was a tall, black woman, whose sense of style always made Janet feel a bit shabby. Sandy had what some might call a quirky personality; plain-speakers would tag her moody. But in the two years Janet had worked for her, Sandy had always treated her well. Still, Janet preferred to keep her sometimes overly-solicitous supervisor at arm's length.

Jay-Jay was a pet name from her father. When he died, there was little left for the family, only a modest pension for her mother. But as far as Janet was concerned, the name, lovingly given, was all the legacy she needed, and she reserved its use for only those with whom she felt a true kinship. Sandy had over-heard her friend, Megan, using it, and appropriated the name. Her boss meant well, but the familiarity grated.

"Jay-Jay, it's so wonderful to see you up and about. How are you?"

Janet could feel the redness rising in her face. Everyone kept telling her there was no shame in be-ing on disability leave, but she found her debilitated state humiliating.

"Hi, Sandy," she smiled wanly. "Not too bad, thanks. Just trying to keep the cabin fever at bay."

"What a stroke of luck. I'd planned to call you as soon as I got back to the office. Ben and I are having a few people over for Christmas dinner, just a few, and we'd love to have you join us if you don't have any plans."

Forcing a smile, she pushed herself away from the car she was using for support.

"That sounds wonderful, Sandy, but I've already promised my friend, Megan, I'd have dinner with her and her folks in New Jersey."

Janet caught the flicker of disappointment on Sandy's face. She had no wish to offend the woman, but the offer had the hallmark of a frontal assault on Janet's Maginot Line. Her guard was up. There would be no breach of her defensive barrier.

"Well, if your plans change, just give me a call, even if it's at the last minute."

Sandy moved closer to give her a hug and Janet's body tensed. She hesitated, then reached out and patted Janet on the shoulder. Then with a wave, she crossed to the other side of the street.

Glancing at the traffic light, Janet stepped off the

curb and continued heading south. The Christmas displays at Bergdorf's and Tiffany's would have to wait for another day.

The office plazas along Sixth Avenue were decked in their holiday razzle dazzle. Even though most were no longer coming up with new designs each year, to the natives—and after twenty-seven years she counted herself among them—the city had never lost the moxie to transform itself into a magical Mecca of commercialism at Christmastime.

As she made her way down the avenue, the succulent aromas from the food carts, strafing the senses, found their mark. At Fiftieth Street, she fished in her pocket for a dollar and handed it to the vendor. Her mouth salivating, she bit into the plump hot dog smothered in mustard and sauerkraut.

"Mmmm," she moaned. "Leo, you make the best dogs in town."

"And you a lady who know her hot dog," he said in broken English, his eyes beaming.

Walking to the retaining wall surrounding a large fountain, she sat and savored each bite. Diagonally across the street, a row of life-sized, toy soldiers in scarlet uniforms stood atop the marquis at Radio City, moving in unison as "Dance of the Wooden Soldiers" blared over the traffic noise. A dose of Christmas and a good hot dog, she realized, made almost anything bearable.

Turning towards the building behind her, she was pleased to see the giant Christmas tree balls at the center of the fountain. She'd loved them from the first moment she saw the sketches laid out on the conference room table three years ago. What a time of highs and lows those five years at Yamatoro USA had been.

"Good morning, Sakamoto-san," she heard herself say. The president would flash a shy smile, say good morning, and sometimes ask how she was doing. To the American staff, he was a veritable saint. The Japanese ex-pats, on the other hand, were treated much as they would have been back home. Their efforts were never deemed good enough, even though they were all too conscientious to give anything less than their best.

In Japan, a receptionist like Janet would have been considered the lowest of the low. Yet, when Janet did not show up for work for three days, catatonic with grief over the death of her mother, they had asked the police to check on her. That act of kindness had pulled her through.

The pain in her back had eased somewhat. As she rose to start the long walk home, she found herself heading towards the building's lobby. *I need to take one last walk around.* The thought surprised her, but she always listened to her gut.

***

Skyscrapers are really smart. She was convinced of it. To Janet, the fifty-two-story, glass-and-stone office tower was a lumbering, lovable giant, from its head, sometimes lost in low-slung clouds, to its subterranean toes, burrowing into the bedrock. Oh, he could be moody, refusing to let an elevator run up his spine or using his hot breath to cause havoc with the cooling system. She was onto him.

As the head receptionist for the building's owners, she'd gotten to know all of the on-site contractors and maintenance supervisors. Whenever they'd offer to show her around, she would pin them down to a date and time.

Everything changed when Mr. Sakamoto was reassigned to Japan. The new president was much younger, but more rigid than his predecessor. She'd returned to work too soon after her first back surgery, fearing that a lengthy absence would cost her her job. Then, with her friends jumping ship and the resulting downturn in morale, she could no longer rationalize holding onto a poorly-paying job.

The next rent hike on her apartment would put her over the edge. Too often she found herself scrounging for any coin or dollar bill absent-mindedly stuffed in a pocket or drawer, with payday nowhere near. It was time to go. Her new job, working the evening shift at the reception desk of an entertainment company, hadn't done much for her social life, but the pay and benefits were better.

Returning to the lobby door through which she had entered, she turned and looked up, just as a ray of light pierced the stained glass of the clerestory windows, throwing geometric splotches of color onto the sandstone walls. *Show off*, she thought and smiled. *I miss you, too.*

***

Only a few spindly pine trees still leaned against the window of the little grocery store. Janet eyed the smallest, gauging its weight and the distance to her front door. What little relief she'd gotten from staying in bed the previous day would be spent by the time she got it to the apartment. She could picture every muscle that would be needed to maneuver it into the lobby and elevator, and the machinations to get it into a Christmas tree stand. A part of her was always ready to throw caution to the wind, but this time it wasn't worth the price she would have to pay.

If she moved very carefully, she might be able to get the artificial tree from the closet shelf. This year, it would have to do.

***

One twenty-seven a.m. *Not bad, Jay-Jay.* Christmas Day had begun with a minor miracle: she'd slept nearly two hours. This might be a day worth celebrating after all. As short as it was, sleep was a gift. No matter how few pills she took for the pain, the side effects lasted for days. Insomnia was the worst.

Easing herself off the bed, she slowly stood up and waited until she was sure of her balance. As she turned the corner into the living room, she reached for the switch on the small lamp beside the sofa. The pale glow was enough to keep her from tripping over the piles of clothes that littered the floor. It was easier than wrestling with drawers and closets crammed full of all the things she never quite got around to throwing away. Marty's things.

March 17, 1978. That was the day she'd made up her mind that he was the man she would spend the rest of her days arguing with. Marty was way too old for her, but he was one of a kind. How many times had he told her that she was his life? "Yeah, yeah, yeah," she'd answer, all the while realizing that he was hers. But he'd mucked it up by getting cancer. Now, she felt her own life slipping from her grasp.

Standing by the large window that stretched from one end of the room to the other, she looked north to the buildings along Seventieth Street. Here and there, Christmas lights blinked in windows and across balconies. In the blackness beneath the lights of the Jersey Palisades, she could imagine the Hudson gliding by. She and Marty had their own way of dealing with the bad times. With eyes closed and holding hands, they would imagine being adrift on the water, weightless, carefree. The river was all the tonic they needed to revive their flagging spirits. Could she survive without that view?

There had been a lot of tears and sleepless nights before she'd sent in the application for low-income housing, but it was done. Whether or not the surgery was a success, pain would be the one constant in her life, eventually limiting her ability to work. All she could do was hope that the waiting list was long, and that she would be able to return here after the February surgery.

The lump in her throat was growing larger, forcing out the tears she'd been trying to hold back. The gentle pressure on her shoulder was what she had been waiting for. Raising her hand, she covered the spot where she felt Marty's hand resting.

Come on, old girl, we can get through this, she heard him say, as he had always done to nudge her past her melodramatic moments.

"Yeah, yeah, yeah," she whispered.

A Redheaded Holiday:
Countdown to a Christmas Hug
Jeff Baird

*M*ost people would not associate Redheads with the holiday spirit. In fact, many, when asked about Redheads, would associate the hair color with stubbornness. (On that we can agree.) Still, I hope that this Redhead holiday tale will help others see that the festive color Red is associated with more than just Santa Claus.

Notwithstanding my robust Redheaded genes, it seems that I am somewhat deficient in other areas. As a result, I have a tendency to fall victim to some rather unusual illnesses. One particular holiday season started off normally enough, but soon took a left turn into Looney Tunes Land.

A key character in this story is the Prince of Redheads, my own Redheaded son, Ryan, who saved my life not once, but twice. The first time he saved me occurred years earlier, during the saddest day in all my years. It was the day I received a phone call telling me that my dad had suddenly died of a heart attack. I was wracked with grief and, unfortunately, many miles away from my parents' home. I grabbed my young son and drove toward their home, with my wife to follow us shortly thereafter.

Along the way, I had to pull into a rest stop, because my grief was overpowering me. Ryan was only four years old and too young to understand that I was falling apart. I didn't know how I was going to live without my dad. As I sat there, absorbed in my pain, my son leaned over and gave me a gigantic hug. At that moment, he brought me back to the land of the living. My son will always get credit for pulling me through that fateful day and giving me a reason to go on.

The second time the Prince of Redheads saved my life was when he was twelve years old. It was the Christmas season and, as sometimes happens in the northeast, a snowstorm dropped several inches of the white stuff in our area. This resulted in the magical Snow Day for students and teachers alike. So, on that blustery afternoon, at the prodding of Ryan and his friend, we traveled to a nearby park. This park is noted for some prime winter activities, and could contract out to "St. Bernard's R Us."

Off went Ryan and his friend, careening down the hills with reckless abandon on their sleds. As the afternoon progressed, they began making fun of me for not partaking in the winter rituals. I didn't really appreciate the fact that my son was taunting me with "Your Mamma" jokes. He was at least smart enough not to make fun of my Redheadedness, since he is a Redhead himself. I believe he knew that I would go all "Chuckie" on his behind, if I heard even one Redhead joke, like "I'd rather be dead than Red in the head," or the ever popular "Carrot Top."

Feeling "My Mamma" being challenged, I succumbed to the pressure to sled down Avalanche Ridge. I grabbed the nearest sled and sped towards the abyss. It took me about two seconds to wonder if this was a bad idea. My initial instincts proved to be correct as I plummeted toward an appointment with the "Red Cross." To my regret, I did my best impersonation of the old opening of "ABC's Wide World of Sports"—no, not the thrill of victory, but the agony of defeat, where the ski jumper flies off of the jump, crashes into the mountain, and falls limp to the ground. In spite of my spectacular crashes, I still enjoyed the outing. However, when we left, I have to admit, I felt a wee bit sore in various muscles. I chalked it up to "I could have had a V8" in my morning routine.

It has always been my experience with being out of shape that the following day is the worst for muscle pain. Indeed, that next day, yours truly woke up one sore buckaroo. Refusing to give in to a little pain, I toughed it out and went to work. By midmorning, however, I was feeling downright miserable. I had to put on a brave face for a meeting with my boss, but halfway through our meeting I started to really not feel well. I decided that it would probably be in my best interest to go home. I was still functioning under the impression that I was just old and out of shape and no longer able to hang with the "big boys," namely my beanpole of a Redheaded son.

As I tell you this story, I have to admit that I have no direct memory of the remainder of the day. So for this part of the narrative, I must rely on third-party sources to tell my story. Thus began the Countdown to Santa.

Tuesday: Twelve days 'til "St. Nick"

How I managed to safely find my way home is still a closely-guarded, state secret. I arrived home at ten thirty a.m., and my wife, Mary, asked me, "Why are you home so early?"

"I don't know what you're talking about; I've always been a Redhead," I replied.

At that, Mary sent me to bed. She checked on me

throughout the day, listening to me mumble nonsensical and incoherent answers to her questions. After hearing me ask for some white paint because I was thirsty, she figured out what I was talking about, and ran to the store to "Get Milk." She knew that it was my favorite drink and always helped me feel better.

By this time, Prince Redhead had returned home from school and was assigned the role-reversal task of babysitting his Dear Old Dad. When my wife returned, my son described to his mother the strange behavior of his father. He also told her that he felt she should call an ambulance and get me to a hospital, because his dad was acting very strangely and didn't even recognize his own son.

In all fairness, our son has a sense of humor and is somewhat of a drama king. What Redhead isn't? He would routinely try to prank his parents in a perpetual April Fools' Joke-a-thon. Thinking that this was just another joke, my wife checked on me, and decided this was just another one of his pranks. However, our son didn't give up and stubbornly explained that Dad normally didn't go around peeing into various kitchen appliances. My wife finally realized that this was no joke and that yes, indeed, an ambulance was necessary. To this day I can't imagine how my son must have felt seeing his father act so strangely and not even recognizing him; he must have been frightened beyond belief. However, he toughed it out and made sure that his dad was okay. My son became a man that day.

Wednesday: Eleven days 'til "Frosty the Snowman"

So, my wife called an ambulance, and thus began my journey into the land of tag team wresting. My first glimpse of a memory of this event was in the emergency room. I must have watched a back-to-back marathon of the "World Wrestling Federation, WWF" and thought I was going to audition for a starring role. Have you ever played tag-team wrestling? Usually there are teammates on a team; my team had only one member, me versus many.

I took on the entire emergency room staff of doctors, nurses, and attendants, and even my wife. I kid you not. I can proudly say that it took anywhere from six to ten power lifters to hold me down while I waged this epic battle. Eventually, they had to put me into a drug-induced coma to calm me down. Sure, it was the only way that those pansies could get me down for the count. Well, let me tell you, I am training for a rematch, and can't wait to even the score, 'cuz right now it reads: Emergency Room Staff 1, Redheads 0.

Just you wait—*it is so on.*

Thursday: Ten days 'til "A Charlie Brown Christmas"

I was eventually diagnosed with viral encephalitis, which is an inflammation of the brain. How so not cool is that? There were two aspects of this situation that are still particularly frightening. The first is imagining what my family must have been going through. The pain and depths of fear that they must have felt during this now not-so–merry holiday season saddens me to this day. Remembering that Christmas was less than two weeks away, I can only imagine the anguish they felt watching me in this state of helpless madness. And to this day, the doctors have only theories of what actually caused this bizarre episode of Howdy Dowdy meets Hulk Hogan, so they can't predict whether it will return at some point in the future. Ho, Ho, Ho!

Friday: Nine days 'til "Checking His List Twice"

I was in a drug-induced coma. The doctors told my family that it would take weeks or months for me to regain consciousness, and that they had no idea what was wrong with me. I don't know if these discussions took place in my presence, but, for whatever reason, I miraculously regained consciousness that very day. I went the remainder of that day and into the night living the second aspect of this nightmare: frantically dealing with having a tube down my throat and being strapped down to a hospital bed. I believe they were taking certain precautions to ascertain if any grudges were held or if anyone was demanding a rematch, based upon my previous anti-social behavior.

Saturday: Eight days 'til "Rudolph the Red-Nosed Reindeer"

The dread that I felt was uncontrollable, and to make matters worse, I couldn't even communicate my fear, unless you looked into my eyes and witnessed my desperate mental pleadings to release me from my bondage. By the end of the eighth day before Christmas, I was freed from my personal hell and able to walk to the bathroom with some minor assistance as I slowly re-introduced my mind to my body.

Sunday: Seven days 'til "Little Cindy Lou Who"

I had returned from Never Never Land, but the doctors were still planning on a prolonged recovery, so my family was preparing to spend Christmas in the hospital. My wife checked with the hospital cafeteria about what they would be serving for Christmas dinner. My kids made sure that we could bring their presents to the hospital and that they could use their Play Station in the luxurious vacation suite that was my side of the hospital room.

To quote a famous line, "I think, therefore I am." I can't explain it, but I recall someone saying that I would not be home for Christmas, or for a very long time. I was still weak as kitten, but I believe at that moment, I began to "think" myself well.

Monday: Six days 'til "Yes, Virginia, There is a Santa Claus"

I was still sore and a bit punked out, but I was continuing to improve and making a semi-remarkable recovery. Later that day, I decided that I'd had enough of all this and announced my plans to go home in time for Christmas. When the nurses and doctors were through giving me the patronizing smiles and nods of feigned agreement, they realized I was totally serious. We had to wait a few minutes for the *Rocky* theme music to fade out of the scene. I was going home for Christmas, and that was that.

Tuesday: Five days 'til "The Stockings Were Hung By the Chimney with Care"

I started to harangue every nurse, and every doctor, and anyone else who would listen to me, and tell them how I had recovered. I demanded to go home in time to see Santa. I told them that if there were any tests they needed to run, they had better do them soon, 'cuz I was going home. Little did they realize the stubbornness of the Redhead they were dealing with, but gradually they began to recognize my determination and slowly came around to my way of thinking.

Wednesday: Four days 'til "You're a Mean One, Mr. Grinch"

The doctors took me at my word and started to test me for every conceivable possibility. They, of course, told me it was routine in cases such as this, but I knew. They were getting their revenge for the Red Storm that tore up their emergency room a few short days before.

The highlight of these pokes and proddings was the spinal tap that was ordered for "precautionary measures." The initial procedure was relatively painless as I endured the "slight pressure." However, as in all matters, the worst was yet to come. Pain and queasiness shortly flooded over me, and I believe it actually delayed my recovery. Routine? Yeah, right.

Thursday: Three days 'til "Jingle Bells"

I have no idea how I did this, whether it was preordained, or it wasn't my time yet, or my Redheaded DNA was winning the war that waged inside of me. I don't mean to make light of viral encephalitis. It was a huge obstacle to overcome. I don't know why, but I just didn't concentrate on that; I was stubbornly obsessed with the thought of being home with my loved ones on the most special of days. I just didn't care what anyone said or did. I was going home. End of story.

Friday: Two days 'til "Miracle on 34th Street"

I have never seen so many stethoscopes at one time in my entire life. They were holding a doctors' convention in my room while they chatted among themselves about all the positives and negatives of keeping me here versus letting me go home. They even occasionally asked my opinion. After much discussion they promised they would sleep on it and adopted the old parental mantra: "We'll wait and see how things go."

Saturday: One day 'til A Christmas Story Movie Marathon

In my favor was the fact that I had a loving wife and family to go home to. I am here to tell you, I am one lucky Redhead. On Christmas Eve, of all days, I was kicked out, er, I mean discharged from the hospital. I feel confident in stating, based upon my adventures upon my arrival, that the hospital was not prepared for the historic battle that would ensue if they denied me the chance to be home for *A Christmas Story* movie marathon.

Sunday: Yea, Santa is Here!

Coming home on Christmas Eve was one of the most memorable events of my life, once I was able to have memories again. However, the memory that I will treasure for a lifetime is when I was able to look my son in the eyes and tell him his dad was okay. I was able to return the love and courage that my son had shown me, and gave him my own special Christmas present: a gigantic hug of my own. He, of course, was probably thinking, "Yeah, ok, but when is Santa going to deliver my Xbox?"

As I remember back to this "Twilight Zone" episode in my life's journey, I am sure that, as a result of my visit to the hospital emergency room, I am now a case study in their training procedures. If you happen to be at a hospital around the holiday season and

137

you hear "Code Red," you might want to pay close attention and take special care to hear whether they are calling for a "Code Red" or a "Code Redhead," because, believe me, it makes a difference. Right, Santa?

Out of Season

Stanley W. McFarland

*Y*usuf hated camels. He hated the spitting and the ill temper. He hated how high you had to sit in order to ride one. Most of all, he hated the smell.

Yet, here he was, with his wife and son. His was one of only two parties in Antiochus-the-Syrian's caravan with a donkey, and for the first time in his life, Yusuf considered that he might be better off with a camel.

The donkey was no longer young, and Yusuf was asking a lot of the beast. His wife, Mari, was pregnant with their second child, and young Yeshua was too little to keep up the pace. Then, there were Yusuf's carpentry tools and camp supplies, and the family's secret wealth of gold, incense and rich ointment. There was little enough of each, but more than enough to get his throat cut if one of the Syrians, Samaritans, or Ishmaelites knew what he had. They wouldn't care about the treasure being gifts from exotic eastern mystics. Yusuf wouldn't believe such a story himself if he hadn't been there to see it.

Last night, the donkey looked to be getting lame. When Yusuf mentioned it, little Yeshua fussed over the beast for a bit. The animal seemed better this morning. Yusuf had no idea what the family would do if the donkey died. Here they were, in the midst of strangers, halfway to Egypt, a place he feared only a little less than this wasteland they were traveling through to get there.

At least Mari wasn't nearly as pregnant as she was the last time they traveled. They had barely made Bethlehem when little Yeshua was born two years before. It seemed a miracle that the jostling of the trip hadn't caused her to give birth on the side of the road.

Many strange things revolved around little Yeshua.

Yeshua was the reason they were taking this trip. Yusuf had dreamed that the king wanted to kill the boy. Why a king should care about a two-year-old child was hard to imagine. Yusuf could trace his line back to King David, but so could more than ten thousand others if the census was to be believed. Yusuf wasn't sure that half that many were of David's lineage. There are always those who claim a royal ancestor to help cover their own shortcomings. Yusuf didn't see why. *Here I am, a descendent of the great King David, and I'm still just a carpenter with a sharp-tongued wife and a bastard son. Whatever that odd stranger meant about Yeshua being of the spirit of Yahweh, all I know is that the boy isn't mine.* Now, because of that boy, he was on the road to Egypt, fleeing a king who shouldn't know Yusuf from a host of other working men in southern Judea.

He had to admit, he liked the little fellow. No, he loved him. Even if Yeshua wasn't his by birth, Yusuf couldn't have asked for a better son. He had a mind of his own and a stubborn streak like other two year olds, but at least he didn't have his mother's tongue—yet. He hoped the child in Mari's womb would measure up to his older brother. Of course, the baby might be a girl. Imagine the shame of having some other man father a boy with his wife and Yusuf's children all be daughters.

Mari had strange, disturbing plans for Yeshua. They could have used a camel, or a second donkey, for this trip, and they had more than enough gold to buy one. But Mari refused to spend the gold and told Yusuf that it was for the boy's army when he comes of age. King Herod couldn't have heard about her saying such things, could he? Maybe that's why they were in the midst of the wilderness with an old donkey and hostile strangers all around. It never pays to stick your head up where the great will notice you. Where did Mari get these notions of exalting the lowly and making the mighty grovel in the dust?

Yusuf didn't trust this Antiochus. In Syria, Antiochus was a fine name, but to a Judean it was the desecrator of the temple, the enemy of the Macabees. They were riding with a man named for the evil king, headed for the land of captivity. All they needed was a neighbor named Haman to make the trip complete.

The donkey balked. It wasn't such a big surprise. *If I were he*, Yusuf thought, *I'd balk, too.*

"What do you want, old jackass?" Yusuf growled.

"He says he's hot and tired and thirsty and wants to rest," said little Yeshua. He said the strangest things at times, yet that's probably what the donkey would say if he could. "Let me down, Papa. I can walk with you."

Yusuf guessed it couldn't hurt to let the boy down. The donkey wasn't moving. "Damn it, jackass, move!"

"Are you sure about that dream, Yusuf?" Mari asked. "Maybe we should have stayed in Judea."

"How can I be sure of anything, Mari? With you speaking sedition at every well, it's no wonder the king wants to kill us."

"Did the dream say Herod wants to kill us, or the boy?"

"I told you," said Yusuf. "The dream said the boy."

"Then it was a true dream. My son will change the world."

Her son again. Yusuf wasn't the father, but she still could say "our son" just to let him feel included.

The boy let out a bray that sounded for all the world like the donkey. The donkey started walking again. Little Yeshua ran over and grabbed Yusuf's hand.

"What did you say to the donkey?" Yusuf scowled.

"I told him there is an oasis ahead, and he'll have figs to eat when we get there."

"Yeshua, we ran out of figs days ago." The boy just looked at Yusuf as if the man was a dullard. "I guess it doesn't matter what you promised a donkey, Yeshua, as long as you got it to move."

The boy's legs were short, but at least he didn't dawdle like other children his age. The boy walked for two hours without complaint. *Maybe he'll be a soldier. I hope not. I want him to be a carpenter, have a family, be happy, and support me in my old age.*

Ahead was an oasis. Three palm trees towered over the little water hole. In front of the water hole was a fig tree. The tree had fruit on it.

Figs weren't due for months yet, and any tree on a caravan route would be constantly picked clean. The leading members of the caravan were already gathering the figs. Ordinarily, Yusuf would expect the tree to be picked bare before he got there, but somehow he knew there would be enough for his family, and even some for the donkey. Little Yeshua patted the donkey and trudged on to the oasis.

What kind of child was this?

recipe for: **Nana's $100 Cake**   serves:

4 oz unsweetened baking chocolate
½ c milk
1 c. sugar
1 egg yolk
1 c. nuts

Nana's Chocolate Cake

Carol L. Wright

Every family has its Christmas traditions, and in my family some of our favorites revolve around baking. We have our traditional coffee cake—the one we all love, but for some reason only make at Christmas. Then there is the red and green cherry loaf that is as close to a fruit cake as any of us is willing to go. And we always make a wide variety of cookies, bars, squares, and balls, without any of which Christmas would seem incomplete.

But above all of our baking traditions is my grandmother's chocolate cake. Nana acquired the recipe from the mother of a friend in the 1910s, when Nana was still a young woman. While my mother was growing up, Nana would make the cake for every occasion: a picnic with friends, a potluck at church, a birthday. She was famous for it. But, for us, it is a treat reserved for Christmas. The recipe, such as it is, has been handed down to every household in our family for generations.

It is a simple recipe with just a list of ingredients and minimal instructions. It goes back to the days when bakers knew the difference between a pinch and a dash. They knew flour was never "pre-sifted" and mixers were spun by hand. Most of us in the later generations have filled our recipe cards with the notes we less accomplished bakers need, but we all adhere to the recipe very carefully because we know the story about our great aunt.

Great Aunt Lilah was Nana's sister-in-law. She was the one who, on my grandparents' wedding day, dressed in black and moaned, "Oh, my poor brother. My poor, poor brother." Needless to say, the relationship between the two women was never warm. Heated, sometimes, but never warm.

Over the years, they competed over silly things. Lilah was Grandpa's younger sister, and resented that his attentions focused on his wife, and eventually their children, instead of on her. Even after Lilah married, she still competed with Nana over who knit better, who kept a better home, and most of all, who was the better cook. On the last of these, Lilah felt she had the advantage.

Nana was a very good cook who always followed a recipe. Lilah, like her mother, was an instinctive cook. She could make nearly anything without requiring directions, and would improvise even when she had a recipe to follow. She was never at a loss for what to make for dinner, because she could make a meal from whatever she had on hand. It was her forte, and she was extremely proud of it. Not surprisingly, she really resented the popularity of Nana's chocolate cake. She tried to devise a competing formula, but never found anything to compare with it. Finally, she asked Nana for the recipe.

Nana wrote out a recipe card for her, as she had done for dozens of friends over the years. The next day, Lilah made the cake, but she was disappointed with the results.

"Dora, you didn't give me the right recipe," Lilah accused Nana over the phone. "It didn't come out the same."

"No, Lilah," Nana told her. "I copied the recipe I use."

"No you didn't. You left something out. You just

don't want anyone else to make your precious cake."

Nana shook her head. "Now, Lilah, I wouldn't do that. I've given that recipe out lots of times before and no one else has had any problem with it."

"Are you saying I'm not a good enough baker to make your silly cake?" Lilah's voice was shrill.

"Not at all," Nana said after returning the phone to her ear, "but you need to follow the recipe precisely. You cannot improvise, or make any substitutions, or it won't come out the same."

"I am still *sure* you left something out. Just give me the recipe again. Then we'll see."

"Okay, here it is," Nana said, cradling the phone on her shoulder and getting out the recipe card. "But remember to follow it exactly."

"I *will.*"

Nana began, "The first ingredient is four ounces of unsweetened baking chocolate . . ."

"Okay . . ." Lilah said. "Um, how much is that in cocoa?"

***

After many years of being told her chocolate cake was the best, Nana developed a certain proprietary pride in it. So, many years later, when women at the office, where she worked as a secretary, compared notes on their favorite recipes, she was certain that her cake would stand up against the challenge of another who claimed she had the best of all possible chocolate cake recipes.

"I hate to tell you, Dora," said Evelyn, "I am sure yours is good, but mine is indisputably the best. I had it once at the Waldorf-Astoria Hotel when I was on a trip to New York City. I was so taken with it, that when I returned home, I wrote to them and asked for the recipe. I didn't know whether or not they would share it, but I figured that if they didn't, all I'd lost was the three-cent stamp for the letter."

The women all nodded. It seemed worth a try.

"So imagine my surprise when, a little while later, an envelope arrived with a return address from the Waldorf-Astoria. Inside was not only the recipe for their chocolate cake, but a bill for one-hundred dollars."

A general gasp ensued, for in those days one-hundred dollars was a small fortune.

"What did you do?" the coworkers wanted to know.

"I didn't really think I had any choice," she said, "so I paid the bill. But I have made a point of sharing that recipe with everyone who asks for it since then. I want to get my money's worth out of it."

It certainly seemed as though Nana's cake might have met its match. Still, the proof of the pudding—or in this case the cake—is in the tasting, so the two women agreed to go home, bake their respective cakes, and bring them into the office for their colleagues to decide which was better. And each one would bring her recipe to share with their friends.

No one was out sick on the day of the taste-off.

Nana's cake sat on her desk, and Evelyn's on hers. They looked the same. They smelled enticing. It was difficult, but the women waited until lunch before cutting into either cake and serving them to their coworkers. And, of course, Evelyn and Nana had to taste each other's.

Nana took a bite of Evelyn's, and let it sit on her tongue. Then, she moved it around her mouth, trying to savor every last nuance of its texture and flavor. It was, Nana had to admit, a wonderful cake. She looked over at Evelyn, who was testing Nana's cake with the same attention to detail. They put their forks down and looked at each other. Neither wanted to be the first to speak. While their colleagues raved about both cakes, the two bakers knew which one was superior.

"Your cake is better," they each said at the same time. Then, realizing what had happened, they broke into a laugh. The tension relieved, they freely agreed that while the cakes were very similar, they enjoyed the one baked by the other woman better.

"Well, I can't tell them apart," said a coworker. "They are both wonderful. I couldn't pick between them."

Neither Evelyn nor Nana thought so, however. They got out their recipe cards to see where the minor differences in ingredients or proportions were. They swapped cards, so each could review the other's. As they read, their expressions changed from curiosity, to confusion, to amusement. The two recipes were identical.

"I guess it's true," Nana said, "food tastes better when someone else does the cooking."

Everyone in the building got a recipe card that day. And since then, in our family, it has been known as "Nana's Hundred Dollar Cake."

A Santa Story

Jerome W. McFadden

The kid eyed Tim up one side and down the other and said, "You are one sorry-ass looking Santa Claus."

Tim thought about it for a moment. The kid was right. The fact that he was sitting on a flattened pile of cardboard boxes between a stack of discarded wooden pallets and a rusty dumpster, smoking a joint, might give someone the definite impression that he was one sorry-ass looking Santa Claus. But it wasn't his problem.

"Kid, you wanna talk to Santa Claus? Go around to the front of the store, take the escalator up to the second floor, and get in line."

"Why you here sitting on your skinny, white ass? Why ain't you working?"

"I'm on my break."

"Taking a toke in the alley?"

"I don't drink coffee."

"I bet smoking weed in the alley don't meet management guidelines for approved breaks."

"How old are you, kid?"

"Ten."

"Who taught you to talk like that?"

"Talk like what? Knowing about 'management guidelines' or about the bad shit that goes on out here in this alley?"

Tim leaned over to glance up and down the narrow back lane to see if there were any other bad characters nearby, besides himself and the kid. But who would mug a Santa Claus? And for what? His red jacket? The ratty white beard and granny glasses? A two-ounce bag of weed?

"Shouldn't you be somewhere, kid? Other than out here in this alley?"

The kid plopped down uninvited next to Tim on the collapsed cardboard cartons, ignoring his sarcasm. "My momma works in the store. Linens and Bedding. But on Saturday and Sunday she ain't got no one to watch me, so she brings me to the store wit' her. We have a nice breakfast 'fore she goes to work and I wander 'round the mall all day. But I gotta check in with her every hour, you know, go by and wave, so she sees me. Can't talk to her, 'cept on her breaks, 'cause that piss-ant manager gets his nose outta shape if I hang around and talk to her. Dumb piss-ant manager. That's how I know about 'management guidelines'."

"Tough, kid, but you shouldn't be hanging out here in the alley."

"I find things out here, you know? They throw away good stuff in the dumpster. Or just shuck it out here against the wall. Broken lamps. Toys. All kinds of stuff. We take it home and fix it up. Good stuff, too."

"Yeah, right," Tim said, not listening. He took another drag and ran the smoke up through his sinuses, and then down into his lungs, and finally blew it out his nose, feeling fine. He did not want to think about another six hours of sitting in that bone-numbing chair with the little monsters screaming at him or crying for their mothers, wetting their pants as they sat on his lap or puking on his shoulder, with the photographer yelling at him to hold them still. All this for ten dollars an hour. He'd rather be back in school. Which showed how desperate he was.

"So, you gonna give me a toke or not?"

Tim almost spit out the rumpled cigarette, "You're ten years old. I ain't gonna give you a toke!"

"It's Christmastime. You supposed to give us little kids what we want. Don't you know that? You afraid that someone gonna see you out here in the alley giving a toke to a ten year old? Like you abusing me or something and it's gonna show up on YouTube? Get your ass fired?"

"Jesus, kid, you got a bad mouth and a worse attitude."

"Get your ass fired anyway, they catch you out here smoking weed on your break."

"I don't do it that often."

The kid smiled slyly. "You won't give me a puff, but I bet you would buy a bag from me if I had one."

"I would not!"

"Only because you think I'm a ten year old and wouldn't have nothing good. Like I'm gonna slip you a bag of oregano, telling you it's good shit and you smoke half of it before you realize that it smells like oregano and tastes just like shit."

Tim frowned. This kid was either old for his age or precocious in a bad way.

"But if I was from a known dealer and be his runner, you'd buy it then, wouldn't you?"

"You from a known dealer?"

"Maybe," the kid said coyly.

"So you got a bag of weed or not?"

"See, I told ya!"

"Told me what?"

"You won't give me a puff, but you'd buy the shit from me if I had it."

Tim pinched out the joint and put it back into his

jacket pocket. His red, polyester, Santa-jacket pocket.

"I gotta go back to work, kid."

"Maybe I'll drop by and see you. You know, in the store. Tell you want I want for Christmas."

"You already told me."

***

Tim saw the kid circling the picket fence of Santa's pavilion. He waved shyly when he caught Tim's eye. Tim ignored him, pretending to listen to the five-year-old girl sitting on his lap who was telling him how desperately she wanted a Bratz doll for Christmas. He finally coaxed her into smiling for the photographer, then pushed her back to her mom, only to have another kid shuffle forward from the long queue outside the pavilion gate.

He saw the kid making another pass. Tim surprised himself by flicking a wave at him. *Why did I do that?* he wondered. *Now the darned kid is joining the line.*

The kid made it just before the lunch break.

"You're a little bigger than the other kids, you know?"

"So? There an age limit to believing in Santa Claus?"

"You believe in Santa Claus?"

"I'm at a bad age, you know? If I say I believe in Santa Claus, everyone says, 'oh, you're too old for that!' but if I say I don't believe, everyone says, 'oh, that's too bad." You know what I mean?"

"Do you believe or not?" Tim said through clenched jaws.

The kid laughed. "You could make it down the chimney, that's for sure. But you'd better take this lumpy old pillow outta your belly and put it under your butt so you don't hurt yourself when you hit bottom."

Tim sighed and resigned himself to ask the obligatory question. "So what do you want for Christmas?"

"How about a toke on your weed the next time we're out in the alley?"

"We've had that conversation," Tim said testily. "Do you want a photo with Santa Claus for your mother?"

"Naw, we ain't got the money," the kid said, sliding off Tim's lap.

Tim grabbed his arm. "Wait a minute," he said, signaling for the photographer to take the picture. The kid forced a smile but then turned to Tim to say, "Why did you do that? We can't buy it."

"Never mind. What's your mom's name? What's your name?"

"Sarah Adley. DeJean Adley. But we can't buy it."

"Sarah Adley? The same Sarah Adley who used to teach at Lynch Junior High?"

"Still does."

"But she's working here for the season?"

"Always does. But we still can't buy the photo. Even with the employee discount," DeJean said, shrugging off Tim's hand and walking away without looking back.

***

Sarah Adley wasn't hard to find, being the only black woman in Linens and Bedding, and the only one with a name tag that said, "Sarah."

"Mrs. Adley?"

She looked up from the cash register. "Yes?"

"You don't remember me?"

"Yeah, you're Santa Claus. You tend to show up every year 'bout this time."

So now I know where the kid got his mouth, Tim told himself. He reached up to take off his red cap and unhook his beard. "Sorry, Mrs. Adley, I forgot I had this stuff on. Tim Donovan. You taught me in eighth grade over at Lynch Junior High. But you probably don't remember me."

Mrs. Adley smiled and nodded. "Tim Donovan. Of course I remember you. You were the first of the infamous Donovan brothers. Tim, Jack, and finally David. How are they all doing? I had David, what, about three years ago? You all three were hell raisers, but in a good way."

"Jack's a senior now, playing basketball for Central. Might get a scholarship to play in college. And David is now a sophomore, also at Central."

"And you?"

"A sophomore at State. Engineering. I just met your son, DeJean."

Mrs. Adley sighed. "What's he done now?"

"He hasn't done anything. Why do you automatically think he's done something?"

"Because Santa doesn't make house calls."

Tim handed her the envelope of photos without comment.

"What's this?" she asked.

"A present from Santa," Tim said with a smile.

***

They found him at the lunch table in the staff cafeteria. Mrs. Adley said, "I wanted to thank you, Tim. They told me at Santa's Pavilion that you paid for the photos."

"You're welcome. DeJean and I are buddies."

"Say thank you to the man," Mrs. Adley ordered DeJean, nudging him on the shoulder.

"I wondered what you looked like without that ratty beard."

"Better looking than you thought, huh?" Tim replied.

"You might want to think about keeping the beard."

"DeJean!" Mrs. Adley said.

"Oh, okay. Sorry," DeJean said, rolling his eyes, "And thank you for the photos."

"You're welcome."

"See, that wasn't so hard, was it?" Mrs. Adley prodded.

"I said 'thank you,' didn't I?"

Mrs. Adley smiled apologetically, "I'm sorry. I am trying, but he is a handful." Tim could see that she was embarrassed that her own son was so hard to control.

"Yeah, I noticed that."

"Well, I have to get back to work. I just wanted to thank you for the photos. That was a very nice thing to do."

"It was my pleasure. A small gift to one of my favorite teachers. I plan to make Jack and David chip in."

She laughed and they walked away holding hands. Tim surprised himself again by yelling, "DeJean."

Both DeJean and his mother looked back.

"My next break is at three p.m."

DeJean smiled and said, "I'll find you."

***

They were back sitting on the collapsed cardboard cartons, their backs against the wall. Tim was surprised how soft the cardboard felt in comparison to that damn chair.

"Momma says you're nice. Your brothers, too."

"She doesn't know us."

"Not like I do, huh?"

"Do you have a smart answer for everything?"

"We gonna smoke some weed?

"No, we're not gonna smoke some weed. Here, I brought you a Coke," Tim said, handing DeJean a cold can.

DeJean nodded, and then softly said, "Thanks."

"So what have you decided on the Santa Claus thing? There is or there isn't?"

"You're the Santa Claus. Can you name alla them reindeers?" DeJean said.

Tim grimaced and said, "Do I look like I belong to the Teamsters Union? They're just transportation. They get Santa from here to there. No big deal."

"Big fat reindeer with no wings, hauling a heavy sled across the sky? Do they shit on the roofs while they're up there waiting for you to come back up the chimney?"

Tim took a big gulp from his Coke and said, "I guess you've decided on the Santa thing. What about Baby Jesus and all of that?"

DeJean's face dropped, as if he had been sucker punched. "I-I don't know."

"That was a tough question. Sorry."

"My momma says . . ."

"Never mind. Listen, I gotta get back to work a bit early this afternoon. What are you gonna do with yourself? It's a couple of more hours before your momma gets off."

"I'm just gonna walk around, you know? Look at things."

"Okay, we'll catch up tomorrow, huh? But no weed. I'm gonna cut that crap out. Okay?"

"Okay, Catch you tomorrow," DeJean said in a little voice that sounded very much like any insecure ten year old.

But instead of going straight back to the pavilion, Tim hurried back up to Linens and Bedding. Mrs. Adley was stacking large plastic packages of pink sheets on the shelves. She gave him a large smile when she saw him coming towards her. "Did he bother you again during your break?"

"No problem. He was fine. He's a good kid."

"He is. Just wild around the edges."

"I don't mind him sitting with me during my breaks or lunch. It gives him something to do and it gives me somebody to talk to."

"That's nice, Tim. Thank you."

"I wanted to suggest, if you want, after my Santa gig is over at the end of this month, I don't mind DeJean hanging out with me for a while on Saturday or Sunday while you're working. With me, Jack and David. He can come over to the house, play some computer games, or some basketball, just hang out with us. We wouldn't mind. I'll talk to them."

Mrs. Adley looked surprised but pleased. "Wh-Why would you do that, Tim? It would be a big imposition on you."

"He reminds me of us, David, Jack, and me, when we were that age. And we owe you. For being a great teacher when we needed you."

Mrs. Adley smiled. "Thanks, Tim. That's very sweet of you."

Tim added, slightly embarrassed, "And I-I think he needs a friend. I think that's what he wants for Christmas. A friend."

Off of the Wagon and Onto the Sleigh

Emily P. W. Murphy

*T*he party was a mistake. A big mistake. *No.* Matt shook his head. The party was an epic, Earth-shattering, life-ending disaster of a mistake.

Matt stood in the snow, looking up at the stone-fronted, Georgian colonial. It was dark out, and the light from the windows was yellow and welcoming. Inside, joyful voices mixed with laughter and music. He sighed, knowing he shouldn't go in. Even after years on the wagon, he shouldn't expose himself in that way. He'd only end up hurting someone.

He looked toward the street. It was peaceful out there. The shops had all closed and the streets were nearly empty. The people were either in church, at parties like this one, or at home with their families, preparing for the holiday. It was hard to believe that, only hours before, the frantic, last-minute shoppers had been rushing around looking for bargains.

He could take a walk—just wander the streets and look at the decorations. This neighborhood had some amazing light displays this time of year. Sure his shoes weren't really made for this kind of weather, but what's the worst that could happen? A couple of blisters and cold toes were nothing compared to the temptation that awaited him inside.

He reached into the pocket of his down parka and pulled out his cell phone. He studied the screen, glowing in the dark, and hit number two, speed dial for his sponsor.

"Matt?" Chelsea's voice greeted him after only one ring. "Where are you, man?"

"Outside—" Matt's voice caught, and he paused to clear his throat. "I'm just outside. I don't think I should come in."

"What?" Chelsea sounded distracted. "I can't hear you. It's kinda loud in here."

"I'm outside," Matt said, louder this time. A couple hurried past him, shooting curious glances in his direction as they made their way into the house. When they opened the door, the light inside spilled into the front yard illuminating the spot where Matt stood. He looked past the door for Chelsea, but couldn't see her.

He frowned. "I don't think I should go in, Chels."

Chelsea said something to someone else in the room. "Sorry Matt," she said back into the phone. "I can't hear you. Bad reception. Why don't you come in? I'm in the library upstairs."

Matt pulled his cell away from his ear to study the screen. The phone had full reception. He bit his lip. Was Chelsea trying to trick him?

He put the phone back up to his ear. "Yeah, whatever, Chels. I'll see you soon." He flipped the phone shut, not waiting for her distracted answer. He had seen the stairs from the front door. Perhaps if he held his breath, and didn't look around, he could make it through the crowd of partygoers and get upstairs to Chelsea without messing up. He studied the upstairs windows, looking for the library. Several of the rooms had bookshelves. One window revealed the flickering glow of a television set, and the window over the front door was blocked entirely by an elaborate Christmas tree.

Sighing, he slipped the phone back into his pocket, and moved toward the door. The closer he got the more the party called to him. He could see the people clearly through the windows, drinks in their hands, and smiles on their faces. They stood in groups of threes and fours. The music, he could now tell, was emanating from a baby grand piano played by a man in a tuxedo. Matt glanced down at his own attire and wished he'd thought to wear a tie. Seeing an out, he studied the clothing of the other guests, but saw that, except for the pianist, everyone was dressed in the same business causal style he had chosen for himself. Matt sighed, his hand on the doorknob. It was not too late. He could just leave, call Chels later and explain.

He glanced back toward the street, but the door opened, pulling him into the arms of a startled woman.

"Oh my," she said, helping him catch his balance with one hand. "I'm sorry, dear; I didn't see you there."

"No, no, my fault," Matt stuttered. Noticing the woman's wool coat, he checked his watch. "Is the party over?"

She laughed; her voice sounded like bells. "Not at all. I just wanted to step out for a smoke." She held up the cigarette in her other hand.

Matt nodded and stepped aside so she could join him on the porch. He felt safer once the door was closed and they were alone. This, he could handle.

The woman reached into her pocket and pulled out a lighter. "Do you smoke?" she asked, popping the cigarette into her mouth. She clicked her lighter twice, then shook it when it refused to light.

Matt shook his head. "Trying to quit," he said, pulling a lighter out of his pants pocket. He clicked it on and held it out.

She smiled, and leaned in to accept the light. Taking a long drag, she released the smoke slowly through her nose. "You still carry a lighter though," she observed.

"Old habit," Matt said, frowning.

"You drink?"

Matt stiffened at the question, but ran his fingers through his hair, trying to act nonchalant. "Trying to quit that, too." He winked at her to lighten the mood.

She laughed. "Well you just don't have any fun, do you?"

Matt shrugged.

"Here," she said, offering her cigarette.

Matt shook his head and smiled.

"No, really. It doesn't count if it's someone else's." This time she winked at him.

Matt laughed and accepted the cigarette, bringing it up to his lips. Taking a long drag, he felt the smoke warm his lungs. Eyes closed, he savored the experience before breathing out slowly. "That's nice," he said, his eyes still closed. He took another drag before passing it back to the woman.

He felt calmer, more stable. Now he could go inside. It would be fine.

With her free hand, the woman reached into her purse and pulled out a silver cigarette case. She popped it open and offered it to him.

"Here," she said. "For later. What good's a party if you can't drink and smoke? It doesn't count if it's Christmas Eve."

Matt considered this. As long as no one got hurt, what harm could a cigarette do? He took one from the case and smiled.

"Take two," she offered, shaking the case. "Really, I don't mind."

Matt shook his head. "Nah, one'll do. Thanks." He stashed the cigarette behind his ear and gestured toward the door. "I gotta get in there."

The woman's eyes narrowed. "Your girlfriend in there?"

Matt laughed. "Noooo, just a friend, but she's waiting for me." He shrugged. "Coming to this party was her idea. It's really not my scene."

The woman laughed. "I hear you." She took another drag, then stepped down to the paved walkway to put her cigarette out.

"You going back in now?" Matt asked, gesturing toward the door.

She pursed her lips. "Not yet," she said, pulling out the cigarette case. "I need one more. I'll see you inside, though." She smiled, a bit of tobacco stuck to one of her teeth. Matt smiled back and turned to face the door. Taking a deep breath, he opened it and walked into the house.

Inside, he was enveloped in warmth. He glanced around as he made for the staircase. The house was impressive, all decked out for Christmas with fires in the fireplaces—there was one in each room—and stockings hanging from every mantle. Green garland festooned each room and wound its way up the banister to the second floor. Matt hurried up the stairs, looking for the library. He found it quickly enough, but it, too, was full. He hesitated in the doorway. There were at least a dozen people inside—each carrying a glass garnished with a frilly paper umbrella—and he didn't see Chelsea among them. He stepped back, ready to make for the safety of the front porch.

"Hey, Matt!" Chelsea's voice cut through the din.

Matt turned and saw her approaching. She was dressed in skin-tight, black leather pants and a glittery, red halter top. He felt his eyes widen involuntarily.

She grinned at his expression and did a little twirl as she reached him. "Nice, no?"

Matt bit his lip. "Yeah, Chels, nice."

She laughed. "It's been sitting in my closet since forever. A couple of years ago this outfit never would've fit but I've lost so much weight since I quit drinking that I thought I'd try it on again. She ran her hands down her sides. "Hot, right?"

Matt rolled his eyes, but said nothing.

"You know it's hot, Matt. You can admit it." She batted her false eyelashes up at him.

Matt smiled. He could never resist Chelsea's charisma.

"It's hot, Chels. Smokin' hot."

She laughed. "That's better. Now, what's this about you skipping the party?" She put her hands on her narrow hips and her lips formed a childish pout. "What were you waiting for, a formal invitation?"

Matt smirked. "I thought you couldn't hear me."

Her eyes opened wide in mock innocence, while her hands remained on her hips. "Not if that's what you were trying to say."

Matt sighed and lowered his voice. "I'm sorry, Chels, but I just don't think it's a great idea for me to be here right now. I'm not sure I can stand all this temptation in one place."

"So I see," she said, reaching up to brush his ear.

Matt reached up automatically and felt the cigarette. He winced.

"I thought you quit smoking."

Matt shrugged. "I'm not smoking it, I'm wearing it."

"And what's that I smell?" she said, taking a whiff of his chest.

"Second hand." Matt paused. "Mostly."

Chelsea laughed. "You weren't about to lie to me, were you Matt?"

Matt smiled. "Nah."

"Well good, 'cause just because you smoked doesn't mean you're going to drink, and I don't want something as simple as a cigarette to get in the way of this." She moved her hands back and forth between them to indicate their friendship.

"It won't," Matt said. "But, Chels, I really think I should get going. There're too many people here."

Chelsea shook her head. "It's good for you, Matt. You've been clean for years now, way longer than I have, and you still don't go out among people. You have to learn to be social again. You can't spend all your time sitting alone, or hanging out with me and other—" she glanced around to see if anyone was listening, "—others like us. It's not healthy. There's a whole big world out there, and you're missing it."

"But look," Matt indicated a caterer carrying a tray full of brightly-colored cocktails. "Mixed drinks are my weakness, Chels. I'm not sure if I can resist."

Chelsea smirked. "You're such a girl, Matthew. Most of us like it straight up."

Matt shrugged.

Chelsea reached out and patted Matt's shoulder. "Don't worry, Matt. You know deep down that you can resist it, and so do I."

Matt bit his lip and shook his head. "I don't know that, Chelsea."

Chelsea grinned. "Well, by the end of tonight you will."

He could see the confidence in her eyes and had to admit that she was usually right about such things. Still, he couldn't shake the feeling that tonight she was wrong.

"Fine, Chels." He sighed.

"Yippee!" Chelsea clapped her hands down on Matt's shoulders and jumped up to kiss him on the cheek. "This will be so good for you. Are you hungry?"

Matt shook his head. "Thirsty," he said, trying to give Chelsea a significant look.

"Oh, let's see if we can find someone to give you a drink then," she said, pulling on his arm. Matt stiffened.

"A ginger ale, Matt, or maybe some orange juice?" She patted his shoulder. "We'll keep you away from the alcohol while you're here. You'll be fine. They have all the good mixers at the bar in the parlor. Come on." She turned and pulled him out of the library and down the stairs. Matt sighed, but followed.

Once in the foyer, Chelsea pulled him into a room packed with people. Matt eyed the front door with longing as he passed it, but nearly tripped over a bystander and forced himself to watch where he was going. This room was warmer than the others, and louder.

Chelsea stopped at the counter and ordered a ginger ale for herself. "What do you want, Matt?"

Matt turned to the bartender. "The same."

The bartender filled two glasses with soda and ice, garnishing each with a sprig of plastic holly.

"Aww, how cute," Chelsea exclaimed, taking her drink and sipping from the skinny straw.

Matt rolled his eyes and downed his in a single swallow. He placed the glass on the bar and turned his back to it.

"Oh, Matt, lighten up," Chelsea said, taking the holly from her drink and twirling it between her fingers. "It's Christmas. Be happy."

Matt tried to smile, but it felt more like a grimace.

"Well, I have to make the rounds downstairs," she said. "You want to come with me, or wait here?"

Matt weighed his options. "Stay here," he said at last, figuring it was better to be alone with a chance of escape than dragged around the house.

"Suit yourself." Chelsea shrugged, releasing his hand. "I'll be back in a few. Don't leave, okay?"

Matt nodded, not wanting to make any promises. Chelsea waved, and squeezed her way toward the door, disappearing into the crowd.

"Hey, buddy," the bartender said behind him, "want anything else?"

Matt shook his head, not even turning around. Chelsea never should have left him alone with so many strangers. He elbowed his way out of the crowd to the next room, which appeared to be less formal than the front of the house. It was also less crowded. Two blessings in one. The television was on, and *It's A Wonderful Life* was playing at low volume, although no one appeared to be watching. Matt collapsed onto the couch and pretended to focus on the movie. Out of the corner of his eye, he studied the handful of people in the room. They seemed so cheerful and carefree. A waiter walked by with a tray of eggnog and they each took a mug.

"Oh look. Holly," one of the women cooed, taking the garnish out of her drink and twirling it between her fingers, just as Chelsea had done. Matt rolled his eyes. *Women.*

He turned back to the movie, trying to ignore the others in the room, but it was difficult when the smell made his mouth water. Without meaning to, he found he was imagining how it would be if he took just one drink, the taste, the warmth traveling down his throat, spreading throughout his body. His eyes flicked back to the woman with the eggnog. Just one drink—what would be the harm?

"Hey, there you are." A female voice startled Matt from his dark thoughts. He looked around, expecting to see Chelsea, but discovered the woman from the front porch instead. He almost didn't recognize her without her jacket, but her musical voice gave her away. She was wearing a shimmery gold dress that was too short for the cold weather and holding a drink in each hand. She smelled like booze and perfume with the faint hint of cigarette smoke still clinging to the curls of her hair. "I figured you'd gone home after all."

"I wish," he grumbled. "This party is a bad idea."

She grinned. "All parties are a bad idea. You mind?" She gestured to the couch beside Matt.

"Actually—" Matt began, but the woman plopped herself down before he could finish his thought. She placed her drinks on the coffee table in front of her and eased her stilettos off of her feet.

"These shoes are killing me," she said with an apologetic glance at Matt. "I'm Sheila, by the way." She held out a hand and Matt had no choice but to take it.

"Matt," he said.

"Hey, Matt. I see you still have that cigarette." She gestured to his ear.

He shrugged. "Savin' it for a rainy day."

"I wish I could do that, but I can hardly resist them." She winked. "So, where's the girlfriend?"

Matt shook his head. "Not a girlfriend, just a friend. She's making the rounds."

"Social butterfly, eh? What a pain."

Matt snorted.

"You know anyone else here?" she asked, wedging her shoes back on.

"Not well," Matt admitted. "I think I've met a few of them, but I'm bad with names. And faces."

Sheila nodded, a serious expression on her face. "She-La" she said enunciating each syllable and pointing to her chest. "She-La. I . . . am . . . She-La."

Matt laughed. "Ma-At," he said, pointing to himself.

Sheila shook her head and picked up one of her drinks. "Look, buddy, I never said *I* was bad with names." She took a sip, her eyes meeting his over her glass.

Matt shook his head. "No, that's true." There was an awkward pause. Matt knew he should say something else, but he wasn't sure what. It didn't help that Sheila smelled so intoxicating. His eyes flicked from the drink in Sheila's hand to the one on the table. "Scotch and a Blue Hawaiian. Interesting mix."

"Hey, you have a good eye," Sheila said, setting the scotch down.

"Lots of practice," Matt said, shrugging. "Why both?"

Sheila grinned. "Why not? I'd have grabbed an eggnog, but my hands were full. And the holly creeped me out."

Matt laughed. "What, you didn't want to twirl it between your fingers?"

Sheila shook her head and moved closer to him, her thigh resting against his. A fresh wave of booze and cigarette smoke engulfed Matt. "Nah, holly has no place in drinks. If they'd been thinking, they'd have given out mistletoe." She met Matt's eyes and raised her eyebrows suggestively.

Matt felt drawn toward her, but jerked back, hitting the arm of the couch.

"Hey, lighten up man," Sheila said. "I didn't mean to scare you or anything. Here." She grabbed the Blue Hawaiian from the table. "I haven't had any of this. It's all yours."

Matt studied her hand. "I'd better not," he said, unable to tear his eyes away.

"Yeah, yeah, trying to quit, I remember," she said, putting the drink on the table and going for the scotch. "Here," she offered him the shorter glass. "It doesn't count if it's someone else's."

Matt bit his lip and tilted his head back willing Chelsea to come into the room, but instead he felt Sheila move closer. He could smell Sheila's scent and hear the liquid slosh in the glass. "Just one little drink," she whispered, her breath caressing his ear. "What's the harm?"

"No," Matt said, his voice weak and his eyes still closed. "Lowered inhibitions are *not* a good idea for me. People might get hurt."

"Yeah, right. What's the worst that could happen?"

Matt tried to hold his breath. "I could lose control and kill everyone."

Sheila giggled and climbed into his lap. "Don't be silly. No one will get hurt." He longed to believe her. "Come on, just one little taste."

Matt's eyes flew open and he grabbed her wrist pulling her toward him. Scotch splashed from the glass as he crushed her body against his, his face buried in the hair at her neck. He took a deep breath, inhaling her scent.

"Easy, cowboy." She giggled, moving back to angle the glass toward his lips. "You don't want to spill it all."

His eyes focused on the glass, and he remembered himself. He stood up so suddenly that Sheila tumbled off his lap onto the floor, jostling the coffee table and spilling her other drink. He looked at the mess, realizing how close he had come to ruining everything. A wave of horror washed over him. He vaguely registered that Sheila was yelling at him; that the people nearby were staring; that more were coming into the room.

"Excuse me," he muttered, jumping over the table in his rush to make his escape.

He elbowed his way to the front door, but found it blocked by a mass of people flooding in from outside.

In desperation, he turned and raced up the stairs, then up a second flight to the attic. There weren't many people up there, just couples taking advantage of the near privacy, but Matt needed to be alone. Spying a window, he pushed it open. The roof outside sloped down past the window, allowing Matt to climb out into the night. He pushed the window closed behind him, then crawled up to the apex, grateful that it wasn't icy.

When he reached the ridgepole, he stopped, taking a deep breath of the cold air. He surveyed the neighborhood below him and tried to focus on the decorations and not on the disaster with Sheila, but his thoughts kept traveling back downstairs. He couldn't leave while she was still there. He would have to wait.

He eased himself down to a sitting position, and leaned against the chimney, tilting his head back to look at the stars. The night was clear as only a cold night in winter can be. He could even identify the band of the Milky Way as it reached across the sky. Taking another deep breath, he willed the cold to numb his despair.

"No one was hurt," he said out loud. But he knew it wasn't true. This had been his test, his opportunity to see if he could coexist with people or prove himself to be nothing more than a monster. And the monster had won out.

He banged the back of his head against the brick chimney, wishing for some relief, but finding none.

He sat for a long time before it occurred to him how very cold he felt and he realized that he had left his coat downstairs. The idea of going down to retrieve it was ludicrous. In fact, the idea of leaving the roof at all seemed impossible to contemplate. With sudden clarity, Matt realized what he should do. He was tired. If he slept here, he would be dead at sunrise.

Matt considered the prospect with the first glimmer of hope he had felt in a long time. All he had to do was remain on the roof and it would all be over. He would be gone, and the world would be safe. He could never hurt anyone, ever again. He smiled at the idea. He reached up and took the cigarette out from behind his ear. Grabbing his lighter, he brought it to his mouth and took a long drag, allowing the smoke to fill his lungs and choke out the last of Sheila's scent from his nostrils. He smiled, for the first time in many months, a smile that truly reached his heart. Finally he knew what he should do.

He smoked until the glowing end of the cigarette reached his fingers, then stubbed it out on the roof, lay back in the snow, and fell asleep.

***

In his dream, Matt returned to the party. He found Sheila, and accepted the drink she so unwittingly offered him. She smiled, and offered him more. The dream was vivid. He could hear her voice.

"Matthew?"

He felt the warmth spread throughout his body, and travel straight to his head. He drank again.

"Matthew!"

He wrapped his arms around her, pressing his face into her hair, smelling that intoxicating fragrance.

"Matthew."

Her voice was softer now, sweeter, more submissive. He moved back down to her neck, to the open wound there and pressed his lips to it, drinking her, feeling the warmth, savoring the intoxicating mix of blood, and alcohol, and nicotine. The perfect cocktail.

"Matthew."

Her voice was a whisper now, so faint he could barely hear it.

"Help."

A mere breath, nothing more.

Matt's eyes flew open. He was not inside. He was not with Sheila. He was not alone.

The young woman lying beside him was not from the party. In his first astonished moment of wakefulness, Matt took in her delicate features, her pointed ears, and her unusual clothing, but noticed more than anything else, how extremely pale she appeared. In the next moment he noticed the smell of blood in the air, and the two wounds on the woman's neck. In the next, he noticed the strange taste in his mouth, not a human taste at all.

Still, it was not until he heard the man's voice that he realized what must have happened.

"Matthew," the man said, "you have been a very naughty boy this year."

Matt turned as a heavy man emerged, impossibly, from the chimney. He was dressed in the traditional red suit with white fur trim. A pointed hat hung down the side of his bearded face.

A vampire ought not be astonished to learn of the existence of another legendary figure, but Matt had to work to convince himself he was not still asleep. He jumped up and backed away from the chimney.

"What have you done?" the man asked, crossing his arms, his expression one of horror and disappointment.

Matt looked at the woman lying in the snow at his feet and remorse washed over him. "I knew the party was a bad idea," he cried, dropping to his knees.

"The party had nothing to do with it," the man said. "The party has been over for hours."

"I was asleep," Matt sobbed. "I didn't know what I was doing."

"That doesn't change what happened." The man stepped down from the chimney and stooped beside the woman, checking for a pulse.

Matt watched the man's face, noticing the tears gathering in his eyes, and he knew what he had done. "I killed her."

The man shook his head, "Not quite. Even *you* can't kill an immortal, but you did something almost as bad. You have ruined Christmas for millions of families."

Matt looked up. "How did I do that?"

The man frowned. "She was my helper. I can't do my job without a helper."

Matt bit his lip and tasted some of the woman's blood still lingering there. "She's not human."

"No, she's not. She's an elf, but she has a family, Matthew. She has parents, and children and a husband, and I'm going to have to tell them what you did."

"I was asleep," Matt whispered, feeling helpless.

"Were you asleep for all the people you killed?" the man asked, his gaze boring into Matt.

Matt shook his head. "No."

The man nodded. "I thought you had improved. It's been years since you've killed."

Matt sighed. "I've spent years alone, away from people."

"That's no way to live."

"No." Matt shook his head. "But it was the only way for me to live without killing. I proved that tonight."

The man gathered the elf into his arms and stood up. "At what cost, Matthew? You now know your limitations, but so many will suffer from what you did.

Not only this woman, but her family and friends, and millions of strangers who never knew she existed.

Matt felt cold tears trickle down his cheeks. "But you said yourself—she's not dead."

"No, but she's also not conscious, and likely won't be for several days."

"Can I help?"

The man shook his head. "I don't think there's anything you can do for her or her family, and I wouldn't expose them to you anyway." He turned away from Matt and walked back to the chimney.

"No, I know I can't help her, but can I help the other people? Can I take her place, at least for tonight?"

The man hesitated, then turned to face Matt. "Do you remember how to drive a sleigh?"

"A sleigh?" Matt looked up and noticed, for the first time, the enormous sleigh parked on the other side of the chimney and the eight reindeer regarding him with gentle eyes. "Sure, I drove them all the time when I was a boy. That was before cars, you know."

The man nodded. "I've seen you on my naughty list for many years now."

Matt winced. "Yeah, I know."

The man shifted the elf's weight to one side, pulled a gold pocket watch out of his coat and studied it. "Look, if we're going to do this we've got to get going. Are you going to help me?"

Matt jumped to his feet to follow. "Yeah, I'm in." He scrambled over the chimney while the man laid the elf out in the back seat of his sled, covering her with a fur blanket.

Climbing up into the sleigh, Matt took up the reins. He hoped that reindeer weren't much different from the horses he had grown up with. "Um, excuse me, Mr.—" He hesitated, not quite certain which of the man's many names he should use.

"Call me Nick," the man said, climbing in beside him.

"Uh, okay. Where are we going?"

"To all the homes."

"You mean all the ones with little kids?" Matt's mind filled with the delicious taste of little children, and his mouth started to water.

"Nope." Nick shook his head. "All of the homes. Come on, Matthew, we're already behind schedule."

Matt urged the reindeer forward. "Where to first?"

Nick pointed to the neighboring house and Matt steered the reindeer in that direction. They took off from the roof and made for the roof next door. As soon as they set down, Nick jumped out and disappeared down the chimney. Moments later, he reappeared and got back in the sleigh.

"Go, go, go," Nick ordered, and Matt flicked the reigns. Soon they were on the next roof.

The town was small, but densely populated so it was not until they were flying over farmland that Matt had a chance to speak to Nick further.

He had many questions, but before he could ask one, Nick spoke.

"Why were you sleeping on the roof?" he asked, not looking at Matt.

"I was waiting to die."

Nick turned to face him. "And you ended up nearly killing instead."

Matt nodded.

"You know the cold wouldn't kill you," Nick said. "So what were you thinking?"

Matt studied his gloveless hands. "I know, but the sun would kill me—" But Nick was gone from the sled when Matt answered, plunging through the air and down the chimney of an isolated farmhouse.

Astonished, Matt directed the reindeer down to

the roof. Before the reindeer touched down, Nick leapt back into his seat.

"What did you do?" Matt gasped.

"We need to pick up the pace Matthew. We'll never finish at this rate."

Matt tried to settle his shaking hands.

"Go," Nick ordered. "Get a move on."

Taking a deep breath, Matt urged the reindeer forward.

It took several stops before Matt felt comfortable with Nick leaping out of the sleigh, and eventually he learned how to maneuver the sleigh so that it arrived at the chimney just as Nick reemerged.

"It was a mistake for you to go to the party in the first place," Nick said later, when they had fallen into a comfortable routine. "You very nearly killed Sheila."

Matt looked up. "How do you know that?"

"It's all on my list. Every good thing or bad thing that you do goes on my list. I probably know you better than you know yourself."

"Your list? Where is that?"

Nick tapped his forehead. "It's all in here."

"Is there any hope for me?"

Nick hesitated. "I can't see the future, Matthew."

Matt bit his lip. "What's your opinion?"

Nick thought for a moment. "I know you don't want to hurt people, but I don't see you succeeding in *not* hurting people."

"Ever?"

Nick shrugged. "I can only guess, Matthew. I don't see the future."

As Nick left the sleigh, Matt felt the weight of those words descend upon him. There truly was no hope for him. He could not stop himself from killing, even for a single evening, and life alone was intolerable. He was sorry, but more for himself than for those whom he had killed, and he was ashamed to admit that, even to himself.

"Why do you go to *all* of the houses?" Matt asked in an effort to distract himself from his thoughts. "And where is your bag of toys?"

Nick laughed. "You actually believe I bring toys to all the good little boys and girls?"

Matt shrugged. "That's what they say."

Nick left the sleigh again.

"I'm not sure who started that story," Nick said when he returned. "But the big kids have it right. The toys are from the parents. I deliver something far more important than toys. I deliver the Christmas spirit, and I deliver it to everyone."

"Excuse me?" Matt asked as Nick disappeared, once more, from the sleigh.

"You ever notice how on Christmas Eve the tree and the presents are just that, a tree and presents, but on Christmas morning they're something magical?" Nick said as he emerged from the chimney.

Matt thought back to his human years, before he was a monster, when he was an excited little boy on Christmas morning. "Yeah, I guess."

"Well that's me." Nick disappeared again. When he returned, he was dressed in a white coat with gold trim.

"Why'd you change?" Matt asked, as he directed the reindeer forward.

Nick tilted his head to the side. "Pardon?"

"Your coat. It changed."

Nick glanced down. "So it did. I appear as people expect to see me. That last family must have expected this." He laughed.

They reached a city and the conversation died. Matt directed the sleigh from building to building barely landing it before Nick was back inside. Matt started getting hungry, and each time Nick returned to the sled, it was harder to focus on the task at hand. He thought of the neck of the man next to him. If the elf was immortal, Nick must be, too. Perhaps if he could just have a little snack . . .

Matt shook his head, clamped his teeth shut, and tried holding his breath.

When they were once more over countryside, Nick spoke again. "What are you going to do, Matthew?"

Matt looked up, startled by the question. "What am I going to do about what?"

"You don't want to hurt anybody, but you can't stop yourself. You're thinking of hurting me right now."

Matt grimaced. "How did you know?"

"The list."

"But I haven't done anything yet."

"Don't you think that contemplating killing Santa Claus would get you on the naughty list?"

Matt closed his eyes and shook his head.

"Open your eyes, Matthew. You need to see where you're driving."

Matt opened his eyes, but didn't look back at Nick.

"If it helps," Nick said, "you wouldn't find me very appetizing."

Matt glanced over at him. "Wouldn't I?"

Nick shook his head. "I'm less human than the elf was. I expect you drinking my blood would be rather like a human drinking glue when he wanted milk. Wrong texture, wrong flavor. I bet I even smell different. Take a whiff, see if I'm right."

Matt took a deep breath. He could smell traces of all the homes Nick had visited clinging to his clothing. He could smell people of all ages, from tender infants to grizzled old men, but beneath that bouquet he smelled something far less pleasing. "Ew," Matt said, looking at Nick. "You stink."

Nick laughed. "Feel any better?"

Matt shook his head. "No, but less hungry."

They rode in silence for a several minutes before Matt spoke again. "What do you need a naughty list for anyway, if you're not bringing toys to the good kids?"

"It's complicated," Nick said pressing his lips together.

"Try me."

"Well, the Christmas spirit comes in a variety of forms. For those on the nice list, the Christmas spirit is fairly simple and straightforward. It's that warm feeling a good person feels knowing that all is right with their world." He sighed. "For those on the naughty list, the Christmas spirit is more complex. It's difficult to put it in words. I guess the simple answer is that if I know where a person falls on the list, I know what kind of Christmas spirit to bring."

They visited another city, moving too quickly to talk. Soon they were flying over mountains rather than countryside.

"So what *are* you going to do, Matthew?" Nick asked again.

"You mean, in general?"

Nick nodded. "I can't let you hurt more people."

Matt sighed. "And I can't promise that I won't hurt them if I'm around them."

"At least you're honest about it. Honesty goes on the nice list."

"I'm usually honest. How far does that get me?"

"Not nearly far enough."

Matt sighed. "I guess the only answer is to stay away from people entirely."

"Chelsea won't like that."

"I'll stay away from her, too. I'll stay away from everyone. Otherwise, in a few years, someone might convince me that I can try again; that the temptation won't be too much. They'd be wrong, but I'd probably want to believe them."

Nick nodded. "It wouldn't be a pleasant existence for you."

Matt shook his head. "No, and it would be a long one, but it's the only way to keep the world safe from me." He sighed. "Maybe you can drop me off on a deserted island somewhere in the Pacific when this is all over. One without any natural resources so no one will ever visit."

Nick pulled his pocket watch out of his coat, and shook his head. "Not until we're finished, and we're cutting it close. You're going to have to drive faster. I need to finish by sunrise."

Matt glanced over his shoulder and noticed that the sky in the east was several shades lighter than in the west. Suddenly, he was gripped with an irrepressible will to survive. He grimaced. "I've got to get inside," he muttered, but Nick was gone again and did not hear him.

They sped through the approaching dawn, the sleigh never landing before Nick was back in it. They zigzagged up and down North and South America, moving ever westward. The sky to the east turned from black to dark blue, to purple and was well on its way to pink. Matt glanced back at the horizon as they raced across the Pacific Ocean.

"How far do we have to go?"

"Just as far as the International Dateline," Nick said.

"I'm not sure if I can make it," Matt said glancing again at the now-pink sky.

"What are you talking about?" Nick said, studying the ocean below them.

"The sun is rising."

Nick glanced back. "Then hurry," he yelled, "I have to finish before sunrise. If I don't reach all the houses the magic will be broken for everyone."

"I can't be out in the sun," Matt tried to explain. "If the sunlight hits me, I'll die." But Nick was gone again, delivering the Christmas spirit to a tropical island.

"*Mele Kalikimaka,*" Matt muttered under his breath

as he angled the sleigh down to retrieve Nick.

They whipped through Hawaii so quickly that Matt couldn't say where one island ended and another began.

"What's left?" Matt gasped as they flew away from Hawaii.

"Samoa," Nick said, his expression focused. "It's all that's left. Keep going south."

Matt scanned the ocean below, searching for the island. He hazarded a glance over his shoulder and saw the pink sky had turned to orange. He only had a few more minutes before sunrise. He faced forward and saw the islands.

"That's it!" Matt cried. "We'll make it." He started angling the sleigh down.

"No, no," Nick roared. "Keep going, that's Kiribati. I've already been there."

"What?" Matt nearly dropped the reigns. "Why?"

"The International Dateline isn't straight. Samoa's on this side, Kiribati's on the other. Go faster."

Matt flicked the reigns, and shouted to the reindeer, urging them to unprecedented speeds. They buzzed over Kiribati and finally Matt saw another set of islands.

"Is that it?" he asked, pointing.

Nick looked where Matt indicated and nodded. "Yes, hurry."

Matt brought the sleigh lower and aimed it toward the first house. Nick left so quickly that Matt didn't notice he was gone until he returned. Matt tried to ignore his movements, and just directed the sleigh from roof to roof. He only allowed a glance over his shoulder as they raced toward the final home. The sky was white on the very eastern horizon. The sun was about to rise. Matt focused on the next house. He had to get Nick close enough to jump. He felt the heat of the predawn burning his back but tried to ignore the pain. Nick jumped from the sleigh and Matt angled it down to retrieve him.

"We made it," he gasped, preparing to leap out of the sleigh and find shelter.

"Not yet," Nick said through clenched teeth. "The houseboat." He pointed to a tiny speck in the water.

Matt didn't hesitate. He took the reins back, urging the reindeer forward. He glanced back and the sunlight nearly blinded him. He turned back to his goal and squinted, through sunspots, at the boat.

He didn't notice when Nick left. He didn't notice when he returned. The sunspots had spread until he was completely blind. All he could feel was the burning of the sun behind him. All he could see was darkness. But he could still hear.

"We made it, Matthew. You saved Christmas."

The darkness became light, and Matt knew the world was safe.

Minerva

Will Wright

*M*inerva's belly was full. She wasn't a kit any longer. She had to hunt for herself. It was good to feel satisfied.

Her den was far away, and she was sleepy. The night was cold and windy. Foxes have thick fur, but she wanted to find a warm place to sleep.

She found a small den. She sniffed at the opening. There was a badger inside. A badger will not share a den with a fox.

Two coyotes were in the dry creek bed. They were curled together. They looked warm. She missed her kit mates. It was warmer sleeping together.

A Christmas Sampler

A rabbit hopped by. The rabbit saw Minerva and hopped faster. Minerva wasn't hungry; she was cold. She let the rabbit go.

There was a clearing. It wasn't like she remembered. The trees were gone. Now there were only stumps.

Minerva spied the trees. They were all lying down in a pile on something tall and hard. The thing smelled strange. It looked dangerous.

The trees looked warm in that tight pile. She would be comfortable if she burrowed into the trees. Her den was far away. She could be cozy right here.

She jumped up on the tall thing, and burrowed into the trees. She was warm. She fell asleep.

After a while, Minerva woke up. Something was wrong. The trees were shaking. There were strange sounds coming from the tall thing. It smelled like fire.

She climbed to the top of the pile of trees. It was difficult. Everything was shaking. The wind was blowing. It didn't feel like any wind she'd felt before.

The pile was moving. It was going very fast and taking her with it. How could a pile of trees run faster than a fox? The tall thing must be a beast—a beast that smelled of fire.

Other beasts like the one that held the trees moved around the pile. The near ones ran with the pile, like wolves run in a pack. The far ones ran past them, going the other way.

They were loud and smelled like fire. Each one had large eyes that spread light like the moon in front. They had smaller red eyes in back.

Minerva wanted to jump. She wanted to run away. She wanted to find her den. She was frightened.

The pile of trees ran too fast. She couldn't jump. She burrowed back in the pile. What else could she do?

188

She didn't like the noise. She didn't like the rumbling. She didn't like the smell of fire. But she was warm in the pile. She went to sleep.

Minerva woke up. The pile had stopped running. She climbed to the top of the trees. The other beasts were still near. Their eyes were open, but the moonlight wasn't shining out.

The stars were very close. They hung from trees and steep hillsides all around her. Most of the stars were white. Some were red or green or blue.

"Merry Christmas," an animal barked. She had seen one of these animals before. It was a human. They were dangerous to foxes.

Minerva jumped from the pile. "Look, a fox," barked another human. "Call animal services."

Minerva ran. The hills were tall and in every direction. They were too steep to climb. Narrow valleys ran between the hills.

Everywhere she went, Minerva saw more steep hills. Humans were everywhere. So were the running beasts, some with moon lights shining, but most without.

There were trees. Trees only grew in the valleys. Each tree was by itself, far from other trees.

There were animals, too. There were squirrels and birds. There were animals that reminded her of coyotes, but they were different.

There were cats. There were almost as many cats as humans. The cats didn't like her but they left her alone.

"There it is," a human barked. Minerva heard a bang. There was a tooth in her side. She ran in a circle to see her attacker but couldn't find one. She fell asleep.

Minerva awakened. She was in the clearing. There were stumps all around. A human was nearby.

"Merry Christmas, little vixen," barked the human. He walked away to a running beast. The beast made a roar. Moonlight shone from its eyes.

She was in the woods again. There were no more tall hillsides and narrow valleys. The trees grew in clumps.

Above her, the stars were far away. Only one was a little red. There were no cats. The running beast went away.

Now she knew the human greeting bark. It was, "Merry Christmas." They didn't harm her, but she didn't want to see them again.

Minerva started walking. She was walking back to her den. She decided it wasn't so far away after all.

Wishing Well Christmas

Cindy Kelly

*J*t was early November, and I was looking forward to our annual trek to upstate New York to celebrate Thanksgiving with my mom and dad. I had just hung up the phone with my mother, double checking on what I should bring for Thanksgiving dinner. As we talked, Mom mentioned that Dad would be going into the hospital the following day for a routine check up after the stroke he'd had the year before.

Shivers jittered down my spine as I relived the day my father had his stroke. He had worked all that day, and by the time he got home, he didn't feel quite right. It wasn't until after dinner, when we noticed him drop a cigarette, that we convinced him to go to the hospital. A year had passed, and Dad was doing fine. Thank God. We all got on the phone to wish him well with the check-up.

A week before Thanksgiving, Mom called back. Dad's test results were in and the news was not good. They had discovered an aneurism in his brain. The doctor told my father he had a choice. They could operate, but there would be no guarantee about the outcome. The surgery would be a second trauma to the brain, like having another stroke. Or they could do nothing and hope for the best, but if the aneurism burst, it would almost certainly be fatal. Neither choice was a good one.

A couple days later, Mom called to let us know that Dad had decided to have the operation. It was scheduled for December third.

"I can't believe this, Mom! Do you think he should have the surgery?"

"He says he'll be fine," she said, her voice wavering.

What if . . . no don't think it, I tell myself.

My family was in shock. We had to prepare to see my father at Thanksgiving for what could be the last time. My son, Michael, who was only seven, knew something was wrong.

"Can we get Papa a special gift before the surgery?" he asked. "I want to bring it to him so he knows we're thinking about him."

"Sure," I tell him trying to hide the tears in my eyes. "What should we get him?"

"I want to go to the collectible store that sells the houses for the village he puts up at Christmas."

The next day after school, we went to the store. Michael searched the aisles, a serious expression on his face. At last, he stopped.

"There it is!" he said, pointing to a high shelf. "It's up there. I see it! That's what I want for him. It will look great in his village."

Michael had found the perfect gift, one Dad would be sure to treasure, an adorable wishing well with a tiny bucket attached.

"Are you sure that's what you want?"

"Yes. He's gonna love it."

"Then let's get it wrapped up in some fancy paper, okay?"

"I want the cool red bow. It's his favorite color."

We celebrated a warm and cozy Thanksgiving at Mom and Dad's. Papa had put up his village. It was a perfect mini holiday town. The buildings even had snow on their roofs. Outside the ground was covered with a foot of newly-fallen snow. Michael and Papa built a big snowman, with a carrot nose, three red buttons, and Michael's new blue hat. It was a Kodak moment, so I threw on my coat and boots and ran out the front door to take some pictures.

The dinner was delicious. Mom had made all of our favorites. We loved the sweet potatoes and the pumpkin pie. Everyone lingered a long time over dessert, soaking up the special memories of a wonderful day and reminiscing about holidays past. Everything seemed normal except for the anxious feeling in the air. *Just pray*, I kept telling myself when the impending surgery flashed through my mind.

When dinner was over, we all gathered in the living room. Michael could hardly wait for Dad to open his present.

Papa took his time unwrapping his gift, commenting on the fancy red bow.

"What could this be? Let's take a look."

"It's a wishing well," exclaimed Michael, "and I'm wishing that your operation will be good."

Everyone had tears in their eyes as Dad said, "My wish is to be with all of you."

It was difficult to leave Dad the next day to go back home. We all hugged him so hard, and told him that we would see him soon.

The next week at work seemed long, and by Thursday morning I was coming down with a sore throat. I had hoped to get back to New York to see Dad again before his surgery, but my father's doctor didn't want me to take the chance of making him sick. Mom told me not to worry. "You can see him when you're feeling better. Maybe you can all come for Christmas."

Sensing the need to take care of me, my husband, Luke, brought me a cup of my favorite vanilla tea and reassuring words. "Your father is going to be all right. He's a strong man, and he has so much to live for."

"Dad's right, Mom," Michael said as he came and sat down next to me, giving me the hug I needed. "He has his wishing well now."

We spoke on the phone one last time before the operation. The conversation seemed light, talking about the coming snow, how cold it was, and how much he loved the wishing well. We didn't acknowledge the thick, dark cloud that hung in our thoughts.

"I'll be okay. Just pray for me, please," Dad said in a soft voice.

"You're gonna be fine, Dad," I told him. I barely hung up the phone before completely breaking down.

Dad was admitted to the hospital on Sunday, December second, the day before his operation. I was so thankful that my grandmother would be at the hospital, too. She brought pillows and extra blankets. Mom packed ham and cheese sandwiches and lots of snacks. They would be staying right there in the hospital, every step of the way.

The following morning, he was taken down to surgery at seven o'clock. Luke had to go to work, but I called in sick and kept Michael home from school, just to be near the phone. We watched television and played some board games while silently praying and wishing Papa would be okay. I telephoned the hospital after breakfast, mid-morning, and lunch. Still no word. After eight-and-a-half hours, Mom finally called to say that Dad was in recovery and that everything went well, but it was still touch and go. They would let her in to see him when they had him set up in critical intensive care. He would have to be very closely monitored.

"Give Dad our love as soon as you see him," I told my mom.

Every hour, we called for updates, through dinner and early evening. Just as we were getting Michael ready for bed, my mother called and said in a voice I had never heard before, "It's Dad. You need to come."

Panicked by the sound in my mother's voice, we packed an overnight bag, got in the car and drove north to the hospital on what would be a very long, two-hundred-fifty-mile drive on the coldest night of the year. I was thankful that Luke drove as I sat there in a trance praying. *Let us get there in time, just let us get there.*

Michael said, "I know Papa will be okay. We wished on his wishing well."

"You're right. He'll be fine." I hoped. "Try to get some sleep, honey. It's a long trip."

"Wake me up when we get there."

It turned out to be a five-hour car ride, which seemed like a lifetime to me as I sat, staring at the snow falling on the windshield.

We finally made it to the hospital around one a.m. My mother and grandmother were in the waiting room when we arrived. Mom told us she had just been in to see my father, and it didn't look good. He had started to hemorrhage and wasn't responding well.

My mother told us that the hospital staff was expecting us, and we would be allowed in to see my father. A nurse came out to get us and led us all the way to the end of the unit to see my dad.

It was a long, cold, anxious walk. We passed families holding onto their loved ones, and doctors talking to small groups in hushed voices. The nurse spoke about my father's condition. My mind was racing so fast, it was hard to take it all in. I didn't even know if I had a voice. I couldn't hear myself respond to the nurse. I just remember being thankful we had made it in time to see him, but nothing could have prepared me for what I saw.

I held my breath as I stared at my father lying there looking like a wounded soldier with his whole head tightly bandaged. His skin was taut making his face look young. The nurses kept tapping his arms and legs every five minutes, trying to keep him awake and making him respond to their questions. When he opened his eyes they were both filled with blood. You couldn't tell they were green.

"You need to stay awake, Frank," the nurse insisted while tapping repeatedly. "Who is this, Frank?"

"My daughter."

I was crying as I held my father's hand. "Yes, it's me, Dad. I love you."

Is this your grandson?"

"Yes."

"What's his name?"

"Michael."

My father wanted to sleep, but the nurses kept right on waking him up, hour after hour. It was a long night as we each took turns standing next to Dad. The nurses let us hang family pictures on a bar over Dad's bed.

There were many other families sitting in small clusters around the huge waiting room. The room was still. One wall was all dark windows, and a small television flickered in the corner. Around the room, people sat with blankets draped over them, trying to snatch a bit of sleep. We exchanged sympathetic glances and a little small talk.

The next morning, when we went in to see my dad, we heard a doctor telling another family that there was nothing else they could do for their loved one. We felt bad for them, and worried we might hear the same thing.

My father's doctor met us outside of the critical care unit and told us that the bleeding had stopped.

My father had stabilized, and was responding to the nurses. I released the breath I had been holding all night long and gave a silent prayer of thanks.

Dad spent three days in critical care before he was well enough to move to intensive care on the floor below. On December ninth, he was put in a private room. The nurses helped him to get out of bed and sit in a chair for the first time since his operation. While there, they removed his bandage, and cleaned his scar daily. He had to wear a light blue cotton hat. He wasn't completely aware of what was going on or I'm sure he would have wanted a red one.

The scar took up a quarter of his head, with thirty staples holding the incision together. It looked sore, and you could see his hair just starting to grow back. Mom nicknamed him "Fuzzy," and got him a new red hat.

Dad's recovery progressed, and in a few days we were able to go home. The following week, Mom got a frantic call from the hospital. They were all aflutter about the new language my father was speaking. Mom told them that he was from Hungary. That explained it. The nurses told her that because of the trauma to his brain, he was reverting to speaking Hungarian.

Mom got a chuckle out of that.

My father had to stay in the hospital for twenty-one days while he went to therapy to regain his strength and relearn his language and writing skills. But finally he was released on Christmas Eve.

We all gathered at my parents' house for Christmas and to celebrate Dad's homecoming. The lights on the tree seemed especially bright that year, and, in the town square of my father's Christmas village, the wishing well sparkled.

"See, Mom," Michael said. "I told you everything would be all right."

"You're right, Michael," I said, giving him a big hug. The wishing-well wish had come true, and Papa was home with all of us.

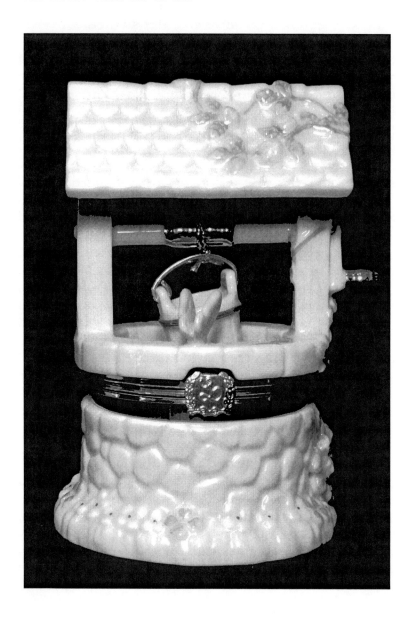

Christmas City Kitty

Sally Wyman Paradysz

J yanked on the large door of my local bookstore, wind at my back, until I managed to wrench it open. *October came fast this year*, I thought, practically falling inside. Looking up, I brushed off my coat. The first thing I noticed was a table filled with Christmas cards.

"Oh, Lordy," I groaned, while I looked them over. "Same 'ole, same 'ole," I said to myself. "Monet, Nature, and more. Oh, Lordy."

It was noon and I headed toward the café, keeping pace with a small woman toting a bulky red bag. She lumbered on as I lingered a moment, distracted by a vegetarian cookbook display. A "veggie" for decades, I was surprised to see so many variations, and made a mental note to come back when I had more time.

Bright red sneakers rushed past me, taking my attention off the display, and redirecting it onto the back of a casually-dressed, familiar-looking man.

"I know him," I whispered to myself. Not being able to place him at the moment, I smiled at the sneakers and pace of his walk. "He certainly is in a hurry."

Moving toward the wonderful fragrance of coffee, I took a seat in the four-chair alcove to the left of the busy counter. Alone for the moment and spreading my belongings on the small, round table next to me, I reached in my jacket pocket for my wallet. Opening it, I saw more than enough money to purchase lunch.

"Perfect." I smiled. The chairs were overstuffed and comfy. This would be a lovely break.

I bent over to retie my shoe when a panicked child shrieked, "She's got a gun!" There was a crash, and people started screaming. I dropped to my knees. The red sneakers ran past and out beyond my line of sight. Not having time to sit up, I heard another loud noise, unmistakably the sound of table displays hitting the floor.

There was another thunderous crash, more distant this time, and the store fell silent. I stayed put. The only sound was the pulse in my ears.

My next move was not brave; it was necessary. I needed to get off my knees. I stood up and peeked out of my corner, into the stillness.

No one was in sight. I was motionless, except for the short explosive breaths escaping my throat. I fought to bring my breathing into balance when something stroked my leg . . . and it was moving. *Oh good God,* I thought. Holding back the scream that threatened to break out, I looked down and discovered a calico cat brushing against my ankle.

I shivered twice before realizing what I was seeing. Two paralyzing green eyes locked onto mine, as if asking for help. Squatting down brought me closer to the stare, and the calico's discomfort.

"What are you doing here?" I murmured. Soft purring was my only answer as she eagerly crawled into my arms. Standing up, I felt a sticky wetness under her soft belly. Dark red blood. "Oh, you poor little thing," I said quietly.

My heartbeat began its ragged rhythm again as I carried her toward a table. Once there, I took a deep breath, turned her over, and looked at the wound. It was oozing blood and other matter, so I quickly took off my jacket, wrapped her within its softness, and held her against my warmth.

"I have to get you to a vet soon, or you'll die."

I gathered my courage and made a beeline for the exit, kitty firmly held to my chest.

"No looking back now," I whispered.

In the parking lot, I saw many people huddled behind their parked cars. I made it to mine, but couldn't find the keys. I checked my pants, and then I reached for the lump in my jacket pocket. Scrunched down on the far side of the car, I reached up to insert the key.

Good news, it opened.

Bad news, the alarm sounded.

"Damn it," I said.

I threw myself in, put the jacket on my lap, and turned the key twice, shutting off the alarm. I started the car, but before I could put it into gear, the back door opened. Jerking my head around, I saw a small girl scrambling in, flattening herself on my back seat.

"Okay, little one," I said breathlessly, "this is not the time for you to be in this car."

"Yes, it is," she said, eyes desperate and wide. "I need to go with you . . . *now*." Her voice began to reach that high-pitched sound of panic, so I made a quick decision and drove off.

Once I was safely away from the bookstore, I looked at the girl in the mirror. Her blue eyes were huge, pupils large, and instantly I recognized her fear. She moaned softly, looking pale, even in her bright red sweater. I reached back for her hand, and she gave it to me. Squeezing it firmly, I said, "Quickly, take the jacket from my arms and put it in your lap because there is a hurt kitty inside it, and she needs your help."

"May I hold her close so she can stay warm?" she asked.

"Perfect idea," I answered back. "Hold her tight. We have to get her to the vet."

"Okay," she said. "I've got her."

"Pretty red sweater you're wearing," I mumbled.
"Thanks."

I drove straight to the vet, trying not to think how much trouble I was in for kidnapping an unknown child. When the kitty went in for surgery, I sat with the girl in the empty waiting room.

"Now, what am I going to do with you, my sweet little girl?" I asked. "We have to call someone." My arm around her small shoulders, I pulled her close.

I waited a long time as she stared at her feet, avoiding my gaze. Finally, she began to cry. We snuggled together, and she soon relaxed enough to speak. The words came out in a rush.

"I live with my foster mother, and yesterday I ran away. She's mean, she's crazy, and she hurts me sometimes. She was the woman carrying the big red bag in the bookstore. I saw you look at her."

"Really," I said.

"Yes. She was the one who knocked over all those tables. When she found me hiding, she ran after me bumping into everything. Everyone was staring at her as she tried to catch me, so when she reached in her bag . . . I yelled, "She's got a gun." People began screaming and running, so I did, too."

Quietly, I asked, "What is your name?"

"Hope."

"Beautiful."

"Thank you. My foster mother has taken care of me since I was three years old. I'm ten now, and hate living with her. All these years, I've been waiting for someone to adopt me. I've wanted to run away forever, but I waited until yesterday. When she left for the grocery store, I took my packed suitcase out from under my bed, and left. The bookstore is only a mile away, so I walked. I fell asleep in the bean bag chair by the books, and when I woke up, the store was closing."

"Didn't anyone see you?" I asked.

"No," she said. "I hid. After everyone left, I ate food from the café. The sandwiches were cold, but I like them that way, and the lemonade was great. I stayed away from the windows, and pulled the beanbag over me for a blanket. In the morning, I hid in the bathroom until I heard people talking, then I felt safe enough to come out.

I asked, "Where is your suitcase?"

"In the bushes outside of the store," she answered.

We talked for another hour. "Would you like to go see how the kitty is doing?" I asked.

"Yes."

I knew Abby, the veterinarian, and signaled her over. Winking I asked, "May we go back and see the kitty?"

"Sure," she answered. "She's going to be fine." As Hope walked toward the back room, Abby smiled, hooking her thumb toward her office door. I nodded, and settled Hope by the kitty's cage.

"Please stay with her for a few minutes, Hope, while I talk to the vet." She seemed to be happy with that, so I left the room.

Walking into Abby's office, I told her Hope's situation.

"I'll take her," Abby said, without hesitation. "Hope can stay with Charlie and me at the hospital tonight. I'll call the police after you leave, and let them know the whole story. Hopefully they'll allow her to live with us until they figure this entire mess out. The police know us well. Thank God for small towns."

"Are you sure?" I asked.

"Yes. In the meantime, we'll trust the authorities to find out more about Hope's foster home situation."

"Oh, Abby, thank you," I said. "I'll go and tell her. Give me a call tonight, and let me know what the police have to say."

"I'll do that," she answered.

"Hope loves it here with the animals," I said. "I saw her watching you closely all afternoon, and I'm sure she'll be fine. I'm headed now for the bookstore to see if I can find her suitcase."

"Fine," Abby said. "If I'm not here, leave it at the front desk."

I brought Hope's suitcase to the animal hospital the following morning. No one was in the lobby, so I left it at the desk, attaching a note to its handle with the only pen I could find. Red.

I wondered how Abby and Charlie were doing as I drove to work.

***

The weeks flew by, and finally my work came to an end. The free time felt wonderful, and I wanted to celebrate. I ate an incredible dinner out that Christmas Eve, and I walked into my home just as the phone rang. It was Abby.

"Hi, Sal, I know it's late, but I wondered if you had a few minutes to come over."

"Sure, it's not that late," I answered, smiling.

"Great, see you in a little while."

I climbed back into my car, noticing the transformation in daylight from only a few minutes before. The snowstorm promised by the morning news had arrived. It was perfect. Small flakes fell against my window, and I smiled, thinking of a white Christmas.

Abby met me at the door, hugging me hard. We walked through the darkened waiting room, and into her private office beyond. There, asleep on a small cot, was Hope, and the calico was nestled beside her.

"What a beautiful sight," I said smiling down at them.

"Good news," Abby whispered. "I wanted to tell you in person. Charlie and I have adopted Hope. The documents were finalized today. Because of all our contacts, and the bruises on her arms and back, they rushed the papers through the system. Hope is ours forever."

"How special for you all," I said, looking into Abby's tear-stained face.

"Yes, Sal, and you have helped make our life complete."

"Oh," I murmured. "She looks so peaceful and happy. For the first time ever, she will have genuine tenderness. I'm so proud of you two. What a precious family this will be."

"Hope fell in love with the calico kitty," Abby said. "She named her Sleigh Bell, and she soon became the inside track to her heart. The rest was easy. She loves all the animals, and the hospital has become her new home."

At that moment, Charlie walked in. He smiled at me, and then looked over at Hope and Sleigh Bell.

"I thought I lost that cat for good in the bookstore," he said quietly. "I found her outside looking lost and hurt, so I ran in to grab a coffee to go. I had her tucked into my vest, ready to bring back to Abby. With all the chaos happening inside the store, she got away from me."

"Oh my," I said. "That's where she came from. I saw someone familiar rush by while I was looking at cookbooks, but I didn't recognize you."

He smiled, put his arm around Abby, and looked at me.

"Merry Christmas, Sal. Your gift was God-given this year, and oh so dear to us."

"Merry Christmas, Charlie," I whispered back. "Merry Christmas, Abby."

Feeling the prickling sense of tears, I closed my eyes, and bowed my head. Slowly opening them, I noticed Charlie's red sneakers.

Santa Claws

Jerome W. McFadden

*H*ave I told you the story of Santa Claws? This is a story of an evil presence that has lived for hundreds and hundreds of years in the very, very far north, beyond all civilization and human reach. It is a man who wears a blood-red suit, and has a fearsome face that is hidden behind a long, matted, white beard and bushy, nearly-impenetrable, overgrown eyebrows.

He comes out of his frozen lair every year on the twenty-fourth of December, to terrify young children. He is guided to his victims by a team of ferocious, shaggy animals with sharp antlers who stamp their hooves in the cold, and who can smell young children from far distances. He slips into their homes in the dead of night, through small openings or unguarded chimneys.

Once in the house, Santa Claws devours any lactate drinks sitting on counters or tables, as well as all baked flour compounds that are carelessly left out on small plates. It is also rumored that he mistreats any small animal, cats or dogs or hamsters or gold fish, that might raise a cry of alarm. His intent inside the house is to punish young, unsuspecting children for mischievous behavior known only to him. He does this by withholding promised rewards if the desired comportment is not followed. A true convert might receive the promised gift, a reluctant follower might receive a reward, but never the one promised, and a recalcitrant victim will have a dirty black lump of coal shoved into a pair of socks, carelessly left around the home.

It wasn't always like this.

Once upon a time, a long time ago, there was a kindly bishop named Nicolas who lived in an ancient European city. He very much loved his parishioners, and was, in fact, upset one winter when he discovered that two sisters did not have sufficient dowries to lure any local young men into marrying them. So, in the dark of night, he sneaked past their house and threw bags of silver coins through an open window. In the morning, the two sisters had a brilliant dowry, enough to bribe any man in the world into marrying them.

Alas, someone saw him do this—the night was not as dark as he thought—and then people far and wide began shouting at him, "What am I? Chopped canoodle? I have no money, and no one loves me, either! You throw bags to the hags, but you got nothing for me?"

Bishop Nicolas did what he could, but it was never enough and the demands never ceased. Slowly he was hounded out of his parish, and then his village, and then his country, constantly driven farther north to escape the incessant demands of an ungrateful public.

After he was gone, the people realized how great the bishop was, and called him a saint. Saint Nicolas. But as he disappeared into the cold north, it was mistranslated into Santa Nicolas and then Sanicole Las, then Santa Claus. But the cold and greedy people back home had turned bitter and mean, and he became known to them as Santa Claws.

And now he travels through the storm-tossed, snowy nights of December twenty-fourth, clumping across

the roofs of frightened children, scaling down their darkened chimneys with his heavy sack of unwanted items, entering their empty living rooms, shouting, "Ho, Ho, Ho, I know what you did this year!"

And the children cringe and cry, desperately trying to remember what they did this year, hoping they had behaved the way Santa Claws wanted them to. But gradually, after years of constant torment and fear, the children finally grow older and learn that the evil Santa Claws can no longer hurt them, and they can ask their parents to buy them gifts, and lumps of coal in socks don't mean anything. They can live their lives as they want. All of which makes Santa Claws even more bitter as he returns into frozen seclusion, waiting for another year for his animals to sniff out younger children whom he can terrorize.

Wisemen

Emily P. W. Murphy

"Mom," my five-year-old daughter's face shines with a delightful smile as she rushes off the school bus, over a snow bank, and into my arms. "I know what I'm going to be when I grow up," she says, her voice muffled by my parka.

I lean back to look her in the face. "What's that, baby?"

She grins. "A wisemen," she says with a flourish.

"A what?"

She rolls her eyes, an expression entirely too precocious for her age. "A wisemen, Mom. You know, like when Jesus was born?"

Clarity hits me. "Did you learn about Christmas in school?" I ask. I didn't know they covered Christmas in public school.

She nods her head up and down several times. "Yup. In Sunday school, yesterday."

That makes more sense.

"We learned about Baby Jesus and Mary and Long John Virgin and the three wisemen."

I stifle a laugh. "Long John Virgin?" I ask, taking my daughter's mittened hand in mine.

"Mom, don't you know about Christmas?" my daughter says, skipping along beside me as we head toward our home.

Clearly, this is what I get for taking my kid to church.

"Remind me," I say.

"Silent night," my daughter's voice echoes off of the neighboring houses. I smile as I hear her sing, even if she only hits half of the notes. "Long John Virgin, mother and child," she croons. I stop her.

"It's actually, 'round yon virgin mother and child,' sweetie," I correct her.

"Uh uh," she says shaking her head, causing her pigtail braids to whip around. "It's Long John Virgin, mother and child. Teacher said so."

I shrug. "Tell me about the wise men," I suggest. She grins up at me.

"A wisemen brings presents to babies," she said. "There were three wisemens when Jesus was born, and they brought him three presents: gold, cents, and fur."

I can't help but laugh. "Cents and fur?" I say as we go into the house.

"Cents are money," she explains as she peels off her coat.

"I see."

"So, when I grow up, I'm gonna be a wisemen."

I consider whether I should correct my daughter on this matter of gender confusion, but decide instead to delight in this peek into her young mind.

"Would you like some hot cocoa?"

***

"How was school today?" I ask my, now seven-year-old daughter as she walks in through the front door.

She shrugs. "Okay."

"What did you do today?"

"We talked about what we want to do when we grow up."

"What did you say?"

My daughter looks at me as if I have somehow betrayed her. "Duh, Mom, I'm going to be a wisemen."

I raise my eyebrows, surprised that, after two years, my daughter hasn't come up with a more appropriate career goal. "What did your teacher say?"

"She said I can't talk about Jesus in school. Why is that, Mom?"

Again a choice, explain to my daughter that she'll never be a wise man, or discuss the issue of school prayer. I opt for prayer.

***

"Do you have any homework?" I ask my now nine-year-old daughter.

She nods. "Yeah, I'm supposed to write an essay about what I want to be when I grow up."

I bite my lip. "And what do you want to be when you grow up?"

She rolls her eyes. "You know, Mom."

"A wise man?"

"Yeah, but I can't say that in school because of school prayer."

I nod, seeing an opportunity to redirect my daughter's plans. "Well, let's figure out another way to say what you want to be. The wise men were scholars. Would you like to be a professor?"

"No, Mom, I want to be a wisemen."

"Hmm, well, the wise men studied the stars; that's how they found Jesus. Do you think you'd like to be an astronomer and study the stars?"

"No, Mom, I don't want to be an astrologer. I want to be a wisemen."

This is turning out to be trickier than I anticipated. "Okay." I try again. "The wise men had to travel a long way to get to baby Jesus. That's why they arrived so late. Would you like a job where you have to travel? Maybe you could say you want to be a travel agent."

"No, no, no." I can tell my daughter is losing her patience. "I don't want to be a travel agent. I know what I want to be. I want to be a wisemen."

I share her frustration. Why does her school insist on forcing children to decide at such a young age what they want to do when they grow up? I put an arm around my daughter's shoulders and steer her over to the couch. "Don't worry, we'll figure this out," I say as we sit down. "What is it about the wise men that you like?"

She thinks for a moment. "Well, I just like the idea of being a wisemen."

I nod and consider how to rephrase my question.

"What did the wise men do that made them so special?"

"Don't you know what a wisemen is?" she asks, her eyes wide.

"I think I do," I say, "but why don't you tell me."

"Well," my daughter says, assuming an air of authority. "A wisemen goes around and gives presents to babies."

"Oh," I say, nodding. "You want to give presents to babies?"

She grins. "Yup."

I smile. "Then write your essay about giving presents to babies."

***

"Mom," my twelve-year-old daughter says one evening after dinner. "You know the three wisemen?"

I nod. "Sure."

"Did you ever realize that wisemen is actually wise men? Two different words? Like, men who are wise?"

I meet my daughter's eyes. "Actually, yeah, I knew that."

She frowns. "I never thought about it that way. I feel so dumb. All this time I wanted to be a wisemen I was actually saying I wanted to be a wise *man*." She blushes.

I pat her hand. "Oh honey, don't be embarrassed. That kind of thing happens all the time."

She looks up at me. "Really?"

"Sure. I was thirteen before I figured out that the nighttime prayer is 'now I lay me down to sleep.' I spent years wondering who Eilaimee was and why I had to tell her to go to sleep."

My daughter giggles. "Really, Mom? That's so dumb." Her expression sobers. "But now I don't know what I want to be when I grow up. I can't be a wise *man*." She sighs.

I put my arm around her shoulders. "Don't worry, honey. You can do anything you set your mind to, and you have lots of time to figure out what that will be."

***

In her junior year of college, my daughter declares her major in business and economics.

"Why economics?" I ask her over the phone.

She laughs the same laugh she's had all her life, though the tone has matured in the last few years. "Well, Mom, it seemed like the wise choice."

I smile into the phone, proud in the knowledge that she knows where she's going in life.

***

My daughter graduates at the top of her class, and before I know it, she has her MBA. She gets a job, and meets and marries a guy I love. I always figured she'd marry someone named Weisman, but her heart led her in a different direction. Together they have two beautiful children.

Now I go to their house for Christmas. I love to sit at my daughter's kitchen table as she cooks Christmas dinner and her children run around me.

"Mom," she says as she puts the turkey into the oven. "Remember what I wanted to be when I grew up?"

I nod as I stir a bowl of cookie dough. "As I recall, you wanted to be a wisemen."

She closes the oven door, and sets the timer. "That was before I realized that they were wise men."

"I remember."

"Well," she says, pulling out a chair to sit beside me, "I'm finally going to do it."

I raise an eyebrow. "You're going to become a wise man?"

She laughs. "Well, not exactly. Actually, I'm going to start my own non-profit. I just got word that the paperwork has been finalized."

"Your own non-profit?" I say, putting my hand on her knee. "Honey, I'm so proud."

"I'm naming it Wisemen Unlimited. We're going to make sure that every needy baby has a teddy bear."

"You're going to bring presents to babies." She takes my breath away. I'm so proud of my little girl.

She grins. "Exactly."

"Gold, cents and fur?"

"No gold or cents—unless of course they're Long John Virgin." We laugh. "Maybe in a few years, but for now, I figure we'll stick with fur."

A Christmas on Nantucket

Carol L. Wright

*T*he mood in the church was somber for the twenty-third of December. Mourners filed out, heads down, and drew their coats closer as they made their way to their cars. Inside, the new widow cradled the urn containing her husband's ashes and fought back her tears.

"Come home with us, Laura," the widow's mother offered. "Brian wouldn't want you to spend Christmas alone."

Laura grimaced. She realized that from now on, people were apt to tell her what Brian would or would not want, and she could no longer check with him to see whether they were right.

"No thanks, Mom," she said, shaking her head. "Besides, I won't really be alone, you know."

The older woman looked at the urn and frowned. "Well, let us know if you change your mind."

Laura struggled to find a smile, but could not. She drew in her breath. "Thanks, Mom, but I'll be okay."

"I'll call you then," her mother said.

"No, please don't," Laura said with more vehemence than she intended. Seeing her mother's expression, she softened, saying, "I'll call you, okay?"

The mother squeezed her daughter's arm and nodded before taking her husband's elbow and leaving the church.

Laura took the urn to the home she and Brian had

shared for a decade and a half. She placed it on the mantle and poured a glass of wine.

"To us, darling," she said, raising the glass and placing it on the mantelpiece. Laura had known this day would come, and thought she was better prepared. She shook her head, blinking back her tears.

She lit a fire in the fireplace, and collapsed in a chair, losing herself in the scent of smoke, the licks of flame, and the popping of the wood. Her mind drifted to the past few months.

It had been a wonderful summer. Brian quit smoking, yet lost weight without even trying. He looked more like the twenty-five year old Laura had married than the man of forty that he was.

They stole away for a week's vacation on Nantucket where they had honeymooned. They spent their days on the beach, dined on lobster, and made love like newlyweds. It was as if the fifteen years of marriage, building careers, enduring miscarriages, and surrendering to childlessness all melted away. At midlife, they felt the joys of youth and health and vigor.

When they left the island, they did what they had done fifteen years before: they each threw a penny into the water as they passed the lighthouse at Brant Point.

"Now we're sure to come back," Brian said, citing the old legend. "If you toss a coin into the water as you pass Brant Point, you are certain to return."

Then, shortly after Labor Day, Brian complained of a dull ache in his upper abdomen that radiated to his back. The doctors ran several tests before giving them the diagnosis: pancreatic cancer. Only five percent of victims survive five years, they said, and Brian would not be among them. His cancer was advanced. He had only three to six months.

At first, Brian continued to work, but the pain worsened. Once a week, he went in for chemotherapy. It could not cure his cancer, but it helped relieve his pain.

In October, he went on disability, and Laura took a leave of absence. They tried to make the most of the days and hours they had left. On good days, they would go for a drive to admire the fall colors, buy apples at a nearby orchard, or pick their own pumpkins at a local farm. On bad days, Laura held his head as he vomited, read to him, and watched him sleep.

By mid-November, Brian looked as sick as he was. He was weak and thin. They celebrated their last Thanksgiving at home, thankful they could spend it together. By the first week of December, they knew that Brian would not make it to six months. They needed to finalize their plans.

"I'd like my ashes scattered on Nantucket," Brian said, then added with a grin, "I wouldn't want to waste that perfectly good penny I threw overboard."

Then, on the first day of winter, the darkest day of the year, Brian died. It was Laura's turn to feel the pain in her abdomen, as if someone had reached in and pulled out something vital.

Laura went through the motions of carrying out Brian's final arrangements. The cremation, the funeral, all went according to plan.

"But now what?" Laura asked the urn. "You weren't supposed to die so soon. How am I supposed to celebrate Christmas without you?" She thought she had used up all her tears, but there were more.

Sleep that night did not come easily. Rising early, Laura went to her computer and made a few arrangements. She threw a suitcase in the car, put the urn in a shoulder bag, and buckled it into the passenger seat. Then she headed east.

Christmas Eve traffic clogged the interstates and choked the tollbooths. The brooding sky gave way to occasional fits of rain, then sleet, slowing her progress. Laura pushed on with only the *thwap thwap* of windshield wipers for company. After nightfall, she reached Hyannis. Parking at the Steamship Authority, she bought a ticket for the ferry. Two hours later, she could see Brant Point Light.

Disembarking at Nantucket, Laura grabbed her bags and walked up the dark, empty street. A cold wind whipped through her coat and stirred the dusting of snow that had settled among the cobblestones. All the shops were closed, some for the season, but a few scattered homes were aglow with Christmas lights. She trudged on to the door of the guest house where she and Brian had stayed twice before. The sound of voices singing Christmas carols wafted from within. She braced herself, and opened the door.

The singing stopped, and five pairs of smiling eyes turned toward her.

"Merry Christmas!" someone shouted. Laura nodded.

"Welcome back," the proprietor said, reaching for registration forms. "I was beginning to wonder if you were going to make it. Where's your husband?" He looked up and caught his breath. "Oh, uh . . . sorry," he said when he saw what Laura carried. A strained silence hung over the gathering until Laura found her room. As she closed her door, she heard them start to sing again, but it was more subdued. She readied herself for bed, laid the urn on the pillow next to her, and fell asleep.

Laura rose at dawn, and pushed the curtains away from windows that were etched with frost. White clouds skidded across a deep blue, New England sky, and the sun glinted off a thin coating of snow. A white Christmas.

Laura joined her fellow lodgers at breakfast. She

bypassed the coffee pot and took her orange juice and muffin to the sun porch. From there she could see the old whaling town decked out like a miniature Christmas village. Why had she and Brian never come in the winter before? It was beautiful.

After breakfast, Laura returned to her room. She put the bag with the urn over her shoulder and went out. She strolled to the beach, now a blend of snow and sand. Standing on the deserted shore, she spoke to the waves.

"Here we are again, Brian," she began. "You said we would come back here someday." She wiped tears from her eyes, and blamed them on the wind. "You said you wanted your ashes scattered on Nantucket, but you didn't say where. I think this is the place." She paused, as if waiting for a response.

She looked at the urn and nodded, then walked to the water's edge. She opened the container and sprinkled Brian's ashes into the receding waves. "I love you, Brian," she whispered as she watched the ashes mix with sea and sand and tears, and fade from view.

She stood a moment, looking out to sea. Then, she felt a fluttering, like a butterfly in her abdomen. She placed her hand below her belt and waited to see if it would happen again.

Her grandmother would call it "quickening"—the first small sensation of the life growing within her. Four and a half months. She had never had a pregnancy last this long. This proof of life was a gift, she thought. It was Brian's last Christmas gift to her. For the first time in days, she smiled. Their string of tragedy had ended. This child, Brian's child, would live.

Laura had wanted to tell everyone about the pregnancy, but Brian said no—not until they were sure that, this time, it was not a prelude to sadness.

Finally, she was sure.

Laura caught the noon ferry back to the mainland. As the boat left the dock, she pulled out her cell phone and called her mother.

"Merry Christmas, Mom," she began. "Yes, I'm fine. . . . No, Mom," she said, her hand on her belly. "I'm not alone. . . . Mom, I have some good news to tell you and Dad."

She smiled and reached into her pocket. And, as they passed Brant Point Light, she tossed two pennies overboard.

The End

About the Authors

Courtney Annicchiarico grew up in New Jersey where she was a high school teacher and a conflict resolution curriculum writer and facilitator. She moved to Pennsylvania with her husband and two children four years ago to be a stay-at-home mom—the best career move yet. "Mis-conceptions" is her first published piece.

Jeff Baird is a career educator at the secondary and post graduate level, and a self-proclaimed computer junkie. He has presented at numerous state and national technology conferences, and has published in the field of educational technology. He now turns his energies to publishing his humorous memoir, "The World According to a Redhead," a book about growing up and living life as a redhead, of which "A Redheaded Holiday: Countdown to a Christmas Hug" is a part. He resides in the Lehigh Valley of Pennsylvania with his wife Mary, redheaded son Ryan, stepdaughter Ashley, and their two dogs, Murphy and Casey.

Carol A. Hanzl Birkas resides in Bethlehem, Pennsylvania with her husband, Gene. She has had several articles published in both newspapers and magazines. Her greatest achievement is a children's picture book entitled *Christmas Treena,* also debuting for the 2009 Christmas season.

Headley Hauser, the star, head writer, and director of the critically *un*claimed local cable television series, *Headley and the Rug*, is still looking to get paid. Though the *Whistleview Penny Supplement* offered to print his series of essays including, "The Cookie Story," "Morom," "John Phillip Souza," and "Look Out For the Swiss," he didn't see that as a path to great wealth and eventual world domination, so he turned it down. His agreement to include "Modern Single Holiday" in this collection came after a long day of stalking Lorne Michaels.

Ralph Hieb enjoys reading and writing paranormal fiction. He resides in Bethlehem, Pennsylvania, with his wife Nancy. The couple enjoys travel, and makes a point each year to take a trip to someplace they have never seen before. In addition to being a member of the Bethlehem Writers Group, he is a member of the Greater Lehigh Valley Writers Group, where he has served as president and a member representative on the board of directors.

Cindy Kelly was born in Rome, New York, and is currently living in Pennsylvania with her husband Mike and her son Michael. She has a Bachelor of Science degree in Elementary Education from S.U.N.Y. at Oswego, is a member of the Bethlehem Writer's Group, and recently started her own book club. "Wishing Well Christmas" is her first published story.

Jerome W. McFadden has held various esoteric jobs around the world while supporting his writing addiction, including selling industrial chemicals in Africa, surfboards in Europe, and crayons in Asia. While his freelance articles have appeared in such magazines as *Skiing, Nordic World, Sepia, Family House*

Boating Magazine, and *Pennsylvania Magazine,* he has also worked as a stringer for various American newspapers (including Allentown, Pennsylvania's *The Morning Call*). He has also been the European, North California, and Mid-Atlantic Editor for *Runner's World* magazine. He is now focusing on fiction, and has won Honorable Mentions in *Writer's Digest* magazine's national contests in 1984, 1990, and 2007.

Stanley W. McFarland was raised in Acton, Massachusetts, and has written dozens of short dramas, primarily aimed at church audiences. He has also written the librettos to three produced musicals, *Acton 1775, Light,* and *Joe and Mary's Rock 'N Roll Jellyroll Christmas Story.* In 2008, a collection of McFarland's poetry, *Confessions of a Protestant,* was published by Marriwell Publishing. He is currently at work on a novel.

Emily P. W. Murphy is a graduate of Lafayette College with a degree in Philosophy. Since graduation, she has worked as an editor both for a small publishing company, and on a freelance basis. She has studied writing at the Iowa Summer Writing Festival, and with Orson Scott Card at the Hatrack River Writers Workshop. Her previous publications include the short story "Should We Do It?" and the co-authored, "Turning Luxury Green: An Environmental Resource for the Hotel Industry." She lives in the Lehigh Valley of Pennsylvania with her husband, Adam.

Sally Wyman Paradysz was ordained into the ministry of the Assembly of the Word, founded in Quakertown, Pennsylvania in 1975. She has served for nearly two decades through spiritual counseling, and ministerial assistance. She has authored many poems for

Lightline, a church-based, semi-annual publication; written a children's book for spiritual retreats; and published a non-fiction story in *11:11* magazine. She is a former hotline, and hospital volunteer, for NOVA— Network of Victim Assistance—located in Doylestown, Pennsylvania. Currently, she is working on the final draft of a non-fiction book manuscript, and continues to provide private counseling.

Jo Ann Schaffer, a recent émigré to Bethlehem, Pennsylvania from New York City, has begun the countdown to retirement. The move has enabled her to rediscover her long-dormant creative muscles. In addition to being one of the founding members of the Bethlehem Writers Group, she has attended the 2009 Winchester University Writers' Conference in Winchester, England.

Paul Weidknecht's work has appeared or is forthcoming in *Oregon Literary Review, Clapboard House, Potomac Review (online), The Copperfield Review, Yale Anglers' Journal, Stone's Throw Magazine, The Oklahoma Review, Outdoor Life,* and elsewhere. He has written a feature-length screenplay, *A Storm In Season,* about a former slave who became the first African-American war hero. He is currently at work on a novel. When not writing, he throws flies to wild trout and gets thrown to judo mats. He lives in northwest New Jersey.

Carol L. Wright is a former lawyer, professor, and pre-law advisor. She is the author of several articles on law-related topics, and of the book, *The Ultimate Guide to Law School Admission.* The stories in this collection are her first fiction publications. She is married to her college sweetheart, and lives in Center Valley, Pennsylvania.

Will Wright, a former actor, singer, and director, has spent the last decade writing. Although he published his poem, "Sadness," in *Poetry Dot Com's* best poems of 1999, he concentrates mostly on children's fiction and songs. In addition to two stories appearing in this book, his story "Figamarroo," and several of his songs, were featured on CATTV's *Headley and the Rug.* His story, "Fall of Brother Moon" received honorable mention in *Writer's Digest* magazine's seventy-sixth annual writing competition in 2007. He lives in Winston-Salem, NC.

Table of Images

CPSIA information can be obtained at www.ICGtesting.com
Printed in the USA
LVOW06s1011261015

459754LV00001B/1/P

9 780989 265010